Fruits from Cana

Fruits from Cana

A Handbook Reflection on Roman Catholic Marriage

by

Richard A. P. Martelles

saint failure's press

Copyright © 2013 by Richard A. P. Martelles

All rights reserved. No part of this publication may be reproduced, stored in a retrieval system, or transmitted in any form or by any means, electronic or mechanical, including photocopy or recording—except for brief quotations for the purpose of review or comment—without prior permission in writing from the author.

Scripture texts not otherwise marked are from the *Challoner Revision of the Douay-Rheims Bible*, published by the John Murphy Company, Baltimore, Maryland, 1899.

Scripture texts in this work marked NAB are taken from the *New American Bible*, revised edition © 2010, 1991, 1986, 1970 Confraternity of Christian Doctrine, Washington, D.C. and are used by permission of the copyright owner. All Rights Reserved. No part of the *New American Bible* may be reproduced in any form without permission in writing from the copyright owner.

Italics within Scripture texts indicate emphasis added.

Excerpts from the *Catechism of the Catholic Church*, second edition, copyright © 2000, Libreria Editrice Vaticana-United States Conference of Catholic Bishops, Washington, D.C. Used with permission. All rights reserved.

By Thomas à Kempis, from *The Imitation Of Christ*, translated by Ronald Knox and Michael Oakley, translation copyright © 1959 by Evelyn Waugh and Michael Oakley. Reprinted by kind permission of A. P. Watt Ltd on behalf of Magdalen Asquith.

By Thomas Merton, from *The Wisdom Of The Desert*, copyright © 1960 by The Abbey of Gethsemani, Inc. Reprinted by permission of New Directions Publishing Corp.

First printing: February 2013

ISBN-13: 978-1482332629
ISBN-10: 1482332620

saint failure's press
http://www.saintfailurespress.com/

This book is dedicated to my wife Gayle,
because it takes two to traverse these dimensions.

Nihil Obstat: Rev. Msgr. John M. Mbinda, Censor Librorum
Imprimatur: Most Reverend Clarence R. Silva, D. D., Bishop of Honolulu

A Note to the Lay Person

Catechism of the Catholic Church—addressing the Sacrament of Matrimony—states:

> Sacred Scripture begins with the creation of man and woman in the image and likeness of God and concludes with a vision of "the wedding feast of the Lamb." Scripture speaks throughout of marriage and its "mystery," its institution and the meaning God has given it, its origin and its end, its various realizations throughout the history of salvation, the difficulties arising from sin and its renewal "in the Lord" in the New Covenant of Christ and the Church. (CCC 1602)

To avoid the many academic explanations found throughout the scholarly annals of our blessed Church, I have attempted to write in a similar voice, a gentle counsel, as that heard in the voice of St. Francis de Sales in his *Introduction to the Devout Life*. As a lay person, I wrote *Fruits from Cana* with lay married couples as the audience in mind. In that spirit, I have intentionally stepped away from a theological explanation of the Sacrament of Holy Matrimony. As the majority of we lay brothers and sisters have a limited exposure to theological studies, if any at all, *Fruits from Cana* explores the mystically rich opportunities of two people deeply in love with a clear, practical, and humble approach to God's Throne of Love and Mercy. The Spiritual Unity of Marital Oneness is a miracle fully accessible when spouses, in obedience to love, grow into that realization that God has intended from the beginning of humanity's creation in His Garden of Eden, and to us now, yearning in that same desire for *Oneness*.

Acknowledgements

I wish to thank Deacon Albert Phillips and his wife, Kathy, and Jo Reyes, Madeline Pruse, Ken Hertz, and others, who read the various drafts and offered their honest opinions. I also wish to thank my friend Bob Wagstaff, artist, who listened to my descriptions and did the illustrations. My special appreciation to Sir Scott C. S. Stone, Knight of Malta, who bathed my original manuscript in red ink, said my thoughts were OK, but my writing "needed help." And lastly to Fr. Tom Heinzel, who accomplished the final edit with such depth and detail. My deepest appreciation goes to my wife Gayle, whose literary expertise helped to deliver me from the 'red' and made my writing understandable. Without her help and love, this book would not have been possible.

Contents

Foreword	13
The Pain of a Wounded Heart	15
Fruits from Cana	17
Husbands and Wives in Marriage	21
The Wedding at Cana, Water into Wine	29
The Soul	31
Singleness of Heart	39
Prayer	43
Grace	45
Devotion	47
Communication	51
Change	55
Peace and Tranquility	59
Trust	63
Fear	67
Vision	73
Faith and Reason	77
Human Sexuality	81

The Marriage Bed	85
Friendship	91
Long-Suffering	95
Encouragement in Trials and Temptations	99
Finances	103
Pleasure	107
Lukewarm Love	111
Competitiveness	115
Meanness	117
Doubt	119
Evil Thoughts	121
Rejection	123
The Pain of Disappointment	127
Anger	129
Vanity	133
Married Image and Appearance	137
Separation and Reconciliation	141
Cultural Differences	145
Children	149
Reading	153
In-Laws	157
Forgiveness	161
Sabbath and Worship	165
The Holy Eucharist	169

| Conclusion | 177 |
| Questions for Self-Examination | 179 |

Foreword

After eighteen years of happy marriage blessed with three children, I found my state of contentment shocked by extreme financial pressure promulgating a two-year separation from my wife, who could no longer bear the worry.

This meditative volume is the fruit of that separation.

For two quiet and somewhat painful years, God gave me the time to reflect on the complex subject of marriage, contemplating the spiritual guidance passed through the centuries by the Saints and Sages of the Church. After reviewing and refining these thoughts for twenty-two years, I have decided to share this prayerful gift with my children and our Holy Church, acknowledging that life is empty, painful, and barren without God's abundant grace; that without the colorful light of virtue, the soul remains in spiritual darkness; that a Christian marriage without charity is doomed to fail.

My family and I are happily reconciled. Faith, hope, and charity made this happen—and these are the virtues others may learn to use in building strong, healthy marriages.

What you hold in your hands is only half of this book. The other half is the experiences and understandings you bring to the words. The questions related to each chapter, found at the end of the book, are designed to help you make connections between the two—with the intent of helping you formulate personal, specific spiritual strategies to give you victory amidst the trials, temptations, and difficulties with which the Devil assails every spiritual union in Christ.

The dimensions of Christian marriage are rich with mystic delights and profound possibilities—and God wants us to be spiritually healthy and prosperous in Him. My wife and I offer this volume with boundless thanks and praise to God for our marriage and with the prayerful hope that the Holy Spirit will use it to further empower yours.

The Pain of a Wounded Heart

O Lord, the pain in my heart is deeper than I can know.
Fiery spiritual darts
disguised in vessels of words
painful
wound and sear my soul in their wake:
her wounded love rejecting my name.
"I will not entrust my love nor my name to yours" said she to me.

O Lord, the pain in my heart is the emptiness
the absence and darkness
of her once colorful and joyful love.
No longer is her love the sweet drink of my heart's thirsty cup.
Her joy grown sad,
her gaiety now dark,
her once heart-filled laughter but a stifled angry spirit–
the wellspring of joy gone dry.

O Lord, spare me your divine assistance to heal the harm I have done.

"Irresponsible!" they said. "Look at what you've done!
God gave you a treasure...
a virgin's pure love,
a precious jewel of a maiden,
for which you have provided no setting, no mount."

O Lord forgive me my sins of neglecting your precious gift...
Heaven-sent love in a virgin of my choice
whose rapturous love transported my soul to delightful heights
and so gladdened my soul,
which is now earthbound in pain and barely there.

O Lord have mercy on us and heal our love
for I will bless her on earth along with gifts from above.

Fruits from Cana

My Dearest Children,

It has been a long and lonely season since you moved to Lake Oswego. Sometimes I try to imagine what the world would be like without laughter and warm hugs, a world seen no longer through the bright, wide-with-excitement, curious, and innocent eyes of children. After asking myself that question, I believe it would be a grim and unexciting place. At times my heart aches with longing for your joyful company. I miss your laughter, your intense involvement with life, your playful spirits and hungry souls filled with love. The joys we once shared are replaced at times now with a dark void, a sorrowful silence. In place of your physical presence, I must learn to be content with recollections of precious and colorful moments. The years we spent hiking through Maui's tropical forests and on volcanic mountains, swimming in her cool mountain streams, snorkeling in her refreshing ocean, and praying to and worshipping our God together: these thoughts are living images burning colorfully in my heart. I will remember you forever while happily thanking Yahweh that He permitted you the gift of life by taking some of my and Gayle's flesh and forming it into your own.

Your mother and I, in our youth and love, were so blessed with each of you as our children: we could not ask for greater miracles—or so I thought. Now, as you approach your teenage years healthy in body, mind, and soul, the once sweet and gentle love your mother and I so fervently shared has been bruised. The pain I feel because of your absence is compounded by this injury in my love for her. Miracles, I have learned, come to those who confirm their struggling faith by praying sincerely on their knees—and spiritual pain is relieved in the same humble attitude and posture.

To help prevent you from hurting yourselves in your own marriages, though they are some years away, I would like to speak to you from my heart. It is from the heart that the language of love is best spoken. Indeed, sacred scripture teaches us, "With all watchfulness keep thy heart, because life issueth out from it" (Prov 4:23). In marriage, unless all issues are understood in a singleness of heart between husband and wife, the spiritual unity is torn, love is bruised, and souls are inevitably injured. Then pain replaces joy, and an ominous shadow of insecurity harasses the gentle peace and love of Christ which once fed and calmed hearts hungry for love. Let your hearts listen carefully to the words being spoken to you: they come forth from my injured and bruised love whose language bears no deceit.

Your adolescent years will bring many changes, both

physically and mentally. Your bodies will undergo hormonal and other chemical changes, passing from puberty into early adulthood. Your minds will expand their horizons of understanding as your experiences broaden and compound. Just as the human body must have a balanced diet to achieve normal physical development, so too the mind and spirit. Feed your intellect with healthy thoughts. The human soul was created to live with and enjoy the noble and restorative truths of God. The soul withers without having these truths for food. You bring divine light into your expanding intellect when you keep and treasure God's sacred truths within your heart. Correct your mistakes as you grow, be sorry for your sins, and seek God's forgiveness. A clear conscience requires an ongoing knowledge about God and His holy Son. With this knowledge, you must also, with sincere hearts, imitate God's love and virtue. A genuine spiritual education is gained when you humbly submit to the will of God. Jesus Christ is the incarnate will of the Father for all humanity, for all time and all dimensions of life. When Christ reigns in our lives, His will becomes our will, His strength our strength, His wisdom our wisdom, His courage our courage, His peace our peace. Our redemption in this life becomes fruitful when we willingly surrender our will to His and begin consciously to live in, with, and through Him.

The Apostle Paul teaches us, "If then any be in Christ a new creature, the old things are passed away, behold all things are made new" (2 Cor 5:17). Allow the Holy Spirit to give you grace in the form of moral courage and strength to obey God in the face of opposing values. To do this, you must read and study God's word—the Holy Bible—daily. Develop and strengthen yourselves spiritually.

Just as you were once infants and are now growing necessarily into the responsibilities of adulthood, so you must move beyond spiritual infancy into mature spiritual decision-making. Committing your lives to Christ is the single most important decision you will ever make. The second most important decision in your life is which person to love and marry: whom you will willingly permit to enter into your life, your heart, your soul, your mind, your emotions, your will, your appetites and desires, your imagination and memory, and, lastly, your body.

Husbands and Wives in Marriage

What are the spiritual strategies needed to secure the unity, the bond, the luminous spark of love so essential to keeping the marital light burning? How does a married couple safeguard their God-given royal treasure of love? It is the purpose of this meditative volume to look back into the history of God's people, and examining illumined thoughts and insights there, to construct just such a defense of faith, hope, and charity as will permit us to grow with the one whom we love.

First, however, it is necessary to gain a deeper understanding of the spiritual nature and activity of marriage—of what is occurring spiritually within the marital union, a state universal to all cultures and so common in appearance. When embracing the marital experience, husband and wife are bound in the development of a unique spiritual identity. They are joined in a miracle of unity of souls and bodies, hearts and minds, spirit and flesh. Lives will be shared in joy and suffering, plenty and want, peace and turmoil. When the Pharisees approached Jesus, questioning him on divorce to test him, he answered: "...Have ye not read, that he who made man from the beginning, *made them male and female*? And he said: *For this cause shall a man leave father and mother, and shall cleave to his wife, and they two shall be in one flesh.* Therefore now they are not two, but one flesh..." (Matt 19:4-6).

These words of Jesus inform us that the miracle of spiritual unity is a divine plan forged by the power of God's sanctifying love. God's love, and only God's love, can assist with the "miracle love" which a husband and wife must have for each other. Also, it is divine love alone which can set the supreme example, the illustration of the kind of love essential in gentleness and, lastly, in wholehearted commitment to forgiveness and charity.

The law of marriage is principally to love: to be one. Originating from the wellspring of the heart, which is the temple of the soul, marital love is primarily spiritual. In the embracing of marriage, husband and wife learn of love from agape, eros, and filial experiences. Agape is God's love, a charitable, untainted, self-giving love that man cannot know unless he gets it from God. The supreme form and expression of agape love in humanity is the Cross. Eros love is sensual, sexual, and emotional. It is motivated by beauty in the eyes of the beholder and by values held by the lover. Filial love is love expressed deepest in friendship: between friends, brothers and sisters, parents and children. The equilibrium of marital love can be acquired only through balanced spiritual development in all three areas: agape, eros, and filial.

Marriage between a woman and a man is of the same

type as that between God and Israel as well as Christ and the Church. The Old Testament prophets rebuked the people of Israel for infidelity, for unfaithfulness, for adultery; these were *spiritual* failings causing the marital relationship between God and Israel to weaken and decay. In the New Testament, we see the apostles telling the people to take as their example for union that marriage Christ has with his Church. In the relationship between Jesus and the Church, we see sacrifice, patience, fidelity, charity, forgiveness, mercy: a bond of active virtue. Christ's agape love—His kindness, purity and, most important, His mercy—slowly transforms fallen humanity into a sanctified "new creature." Scripture doesn't say that the husband should be like Christ and the wife like the Church, but that the souls of the two should hold themselves and exercise themselves in the same type of relationship which binds Christ and His Church. Like Jesus and the Church, husband and wife see one another's weaknesses and love each other through and in spite of those weaknesses. They build each other up in virtue—and the more they exercise various virtues, the more God grants them because those virtues are necessary for the ushering in of His kingdom. Like Christ and His Church, in mercy and fidelity, wife and husband love each other into sainthood.

The lesson here is the bond of love achieved through a healthy marriage—mirroring the unity that Christ has with His Bride, the Church, and, most important, His mercy with and for Her throughout the whole mysterious affair of reconciliation and redemption. Consider how the agape love of Jesus slowly transforms the Church's fallen humanity, residing still in a state of rebellion, into a sanctified obedience and true joy. Witness how the Bride's—humanity's—sinful actions have been and still are being transformed into a humble submission to His will: how rebellious flesh is being reconciled—gently drawn—into a life with a new and humbled spirit surrendering in freedom and joy to God.

Correspondingly, then, see how the sinfully complex man and woman can be drawn into living a life of spiritual simplicity and humility. Study how truth assumes its rightful role with humanity while falsehood and self-love die when the soul is made healthy with the fruits of discipline. Marital love becomes as God intended: that unique spiritual experience through which a man and woman can learn to fully experience life and virgin-like hearts, fed by the pure love of God which gradually transforms the two into His likeness.

Saint Chrysostom, who died in A.D. 407, truthfully stated that human relations in marriage bring an end to virginity but, by being baptized in Christ, virginity and innocence are restored. And a few years later, Saint Augustine of Hippo, who passed away in A.D. 430, expanded on that thought by stating that virginity of the flesh is bodily integrity, while virginity of the heart is a faith that is unblemished and held pure for God and the other.

Husband and wife lose their fleshly virginity in marriage but are presented with the opportunity for taking their hearts back to a virgin state. Virginity of the heart means keeping one's heart pure. In a spiritually ignorant marriage, a husband and wife may not physically transgress against one another but may go about with hidden thoughts, indulging in impure thoughts within themselves and playing subtle games on the surface. In a committed Christian marriage, however, husband and wife can help each other toward spiritual virginity by practicing a life of virtue towards each other, refusing to play the games of the world within their hearts. The virtue they have for each other draws their hearts back to a pure and balanced state.

Marriage is a gift whereby husband and wife are granted the divine opportunity to learn of love in the full dimension of its joys and sorrows, ecstasies and agonies, hope and despair. The marital union assists the spouses in developing knowledge and wisdom and prompts them to move forward or fall back to reassess their path while on their way home to the Father. Marriage is a divine gift which demands total responsibility and moral courage when all seems pragmatically impossible. Christ in His love never loses faith in His people, the Church. In spite of their weaknesses, lack of faith, dim hopes, laziness, and sins, His holiness keeps Him in Oneness with His Bride. Likewise, husbands and wives must, with generous effort, keep their blessing, the gift of marriage, "glorious..., not having spot or wrinkle" (Eph 5:27).

It is commonly agreed by those who have studied the book of Job that Job says the life of man upon earth is a continual warfare. No matter how far we have advanced in our spiritual life, we must never expect immunity from trials, tribulations, and emotional ups and downs. So it is with marriage. No matter how much love a husband has for his wife or she for him, each as a developing individual must be on constant guard, never expecting immunity from temptations, distractions, lukewarmness, and other assaults which attempt to put asunder what God has joined together.

Marriage in a spiritual way has its own climate conditions. Sometimes the marital atmosphere is charged with negative emotions and uncertain outlooks. On other occasions, it is joyful, warm with love, and peaceful. Learn to be prayerfully patient when emotional conflicts threaten and afflict your marital harmony. As with the weather, storms do not last forever: so too will your joy return. As pessimistic as we can become over the weather, we must never be pessimistic about God's love for us or His ability and desire to assist us in our trials and problems. Marriage provides a man and woman with the opportunity to engage in a practical mystery of love. It is both a sacred and pragmatic affair: a sanctified state emotionally charged with down-to-earth realities such as impatience or unnecessary anger. When our problems appear beyond solution, we must seek Him, the Divine Healer, to renew our joy and keep our spirits willing and divinely balanced.

As a person—husband or wife—you were created with a high destiny: "For God created man incorruptible, and to the image of his own likeness he made him" (Wis 2:23). You were created a living and distinct expression of His love, His virtue, His knowledge and wisdom. He provided you with His image to share His name, His holiness, His truth, His joys, and the bountiful glory of His creation. He provided you with a memory to recall His saving merciful deeds for people and the delights of those who walk in the love and law of the Lord.

Consider that God loved you so much He granted you a unique life of love to experience. In marriage, you are permitted by His word to become one with another human being: to drink from the same cup of life; to share with oneness the emotions of the heart, the groanings of the spirit, and the sanctified joys of the flesh. The noble destiny of marriage is planted in human practicality, cultivated in devotion, enriched with the gifts of the spirit, and harvested in mystical glory. Consider the benefits with which He has blessed you and consecrate your marriage to Him with thanksgiving.

There is only one pure power which, with the spouses' cooperation, keeps a marriage united. This power belongs neither to husband or wife, but to God: charity, mercy, forgiveness, truth, and joy are the powers which maintain marital unity. Practice charity with each other, and its power will overrule the plague of excuses, feeble reasonings, and selfish love which fester from fallen humanity. Marriage is a gift of divine opportunities working miracles of reconciliation and redemption within the many weaknesses of the human family. Paraphrasing the Psalmist (Psalm 100), remember that it is He who made us and not we ourselves.

The Sacrament of Matrimony presents a husband and wife with sacred opportunities whereby love purifies their thoughts and practical actions. Thus the "common" and universal state of marriage can become a doorway into a deep and genuine spirituality—into the Presence of God. Yet this glorious destiny is coupled with the complexity and myriad weaknesses of two uncertain and developing human beings. A husband and wife encounter doubts, financial pressures, fears, and anguish because of each other. At times, finding God's charity in a painfully dark situation is like trying to find a cascading waterfall with a cool running stream amidst the full heat of a treeless desert. How then can a wife and husband prepare and take stock to defend the rarest of treasures, their marriage, against assault by a host of enigmatic problems which threaten to split what God has joined together? Ensuing chapters of this small volume explore some spiritual and practical answers.

The Wedding at Cana, Water into Wine

> His mother saith to the waiters: Whatsoever he shall say to you, do ye....Jesus saith to them: Fill the waterpots with water. And they filled them up to the brim. And Jesus saith to them: Draw out now, and carry to the chief steward of the feast. And they carried it. And when the chief steward had tasted the water made wine, and knew not whence it was, but the waiters knew who had drawn the water; the chief steward calleth the bridegroom, And saith to him: Every man at first setteth forth good wine, and when men have well drunk, then that which is worse. But thou hast kept the good wine until now. This beginning of miracles did Jesus in Cana of Galilee; and manifested his glory, and his disciples believed in him. (John 2:5, 7-11)

The symbolism here is mystically rich and parallels Christ's relationship with His Bride, the Church. Christ has accepted (transformed) countless numbers of penitent lives, turning sinners into saints, water into wine, in order to establish and sustain a relationship with His Beloved, the Church. If He can receive an empty and broken human life and mend it, healing it to where it is filled with His merciful glory, can He not take an empty and broken marriage and restore it with the glory of love's goods?

Do "[w]hatsoever he shall say to you," His Blessed Mother said. If we live His Gospel, our ordinary and empty lives will be filled with wine: the love of His Holy Spirit. By listening to what He tells us, our earthly, ordinary, and common thoughts on the subject of matrimony are strengthened by the day-to-day presence of divine love turning our "water into wine." By having faith in what He tells us, we can see the eternal power of Christ's love performing yet another miracle, as in our lives He "manifest[s] his glory" (John 2:11).

Christian marriage is just as much a mystery and miracle as that of Christ and His Bride, the Church. It is He who receives the willingness of the empty in spirit and fills them with the richness of His glory. Offer Him the ordinary water of your marriage—your problems and impatience, misunderstandings and disappointments—and humbly behold the gradual miracle of His turning it into wine, rich in the gifts of love.

The Soul

> Bless the Lord, O my soul:
> and let all that is within me bless his holy name.
> Bless the Lord, O my soul,
> and never forget all he hath done for thee...
>
> Bless the Lord, all his works:
> in every place of his dominion,
> O my soul, bless thou the Lord. (Ps 102:1-2, 22)[1]

Mindful of the fact that Jesus Christ turned water into the wine at Cana and that history is filled with examples of ordinary and sometimes very sinful lives transformed into sainthood, I would like to consider with you the issue of our souls. For if we, too, wish to be converted from the water state of being to the wine state of sainthood, we must understand what is the "soul" God asks from us in exchange for that which He offers to us.

For many Christians, the soul is a nebulous spiritual "something," the reality of which is accepted but never defined. Some say "it" is a part of man which continues to

---

[1] In the Latin Vulgate and the Douay-Rheims, this Psalm is numbered 102. In more recent translations, this Psalm is numbered 103.

live after the body dies. Others say "it" is the spirit. Some do not know. Ask yourself, "What is the soul? What is its makeup? What is its function?" And most important, "What is its relationship to God and its purpose within every human being?"

What is the soul? We expect the soul to be something mysterious and complex. It is, and it is not. The soul is standard to all humanity; it is the basic spiritual organism within every human being. As such, it performs a dynamic chronicling of every thought, good and evil, every prayer and unintelligible spiritual groan. It records each sinful act, each good deed and laugh, each worry, concern, and tear of sadness. The soul is to the body what film is to the camcorder. Film records whatever passes before the lens of the camcorder; correspondingly, your soul is a spiritual living recording film which captures all human life in its animation.

What is the makeup of the soul? According to the teachings of St. John of the Cross (A.D. 1542-1591), the Mystical Doctor of the Church, the soul comprises the heart, the intellect, imagination and memory, emotions, free will, and appetites and desires. These faculties, functioning together in the fallen state, are the likeness and image of unredeemed man. Through the process of rebirth, the soul's faculties are redeemed, and the soul gradually transformed into the likeness and image of Christ, the Anointed One.

What is the soul's function? The soul is that creation God

performs which makes human beings human—which gives a person the capacity to be the image and likeness of God Himself. A soul is God's agent in the whole process of reconciliation and redemption. God creates life, bestows this life—and you come into the world as a living soul. Exposed to good and evil, you begin to exercise what St. John of the Cross has identified as the faculties of the soul: the heart, the intellect, imagination and memory, emotions, free will, and appetites and desires. You apply everything you are as a human being in responding to the magnetisms—influences—of good and evil.

Then as you grow into an understanding of your need for salvation, recognizing the aspects of sin permeating your life, you begin applying (disciplining) your soul's faculties in the way that is comparable with Who He is as God in likeness and image: aligning your heart, intellect, etc. with His likeness and image. You direct your intelligence toward wisdom, your heart toward purity, your free will toward the divine will, your emotions toward stability, the appetites and desires toward moderation. Yet you are still a separate individual—a uniquely thumbprinted, distinctly identifiable person—but in the image and likeness of God because your soul is responding to His call and will in life.

In order to use this soul to come to the conformity of an identity which is in the likeness and image of God, you have to live the life of love. Love must operate through your soul: it has to operate through your intellect, through your emotions, your free will, your appetite and desires, etc. When you begin to apply all the soul's faculties to the laws of love, you then start to conform that fallen identity of man into that which is the identity of the Anointed One's image—the *Redeemer,* who is Jesus Christ. So it is your soul that brings you back into the Likeness and the Image; and as you come back, you as a person—a separate person—bring this identity into your humanity. In other words, you transform your human identity into one which is more and more Christlike. This whole process is you, in and with and through the Holy Spirit, taking the various faculties of your soul through transformation—you slowly reconciling the fallen life of your soul to that of God's will—remembering always that God gave you those faculties through which you are able to resemble Him in your daily life as a human being.

Souls may be pictured as cells of God, each carrying the spiritual genes and DNA of their Creator. As these human souls come into being—born as infants, maturing through puberty and into adulthood—they should be living the life God originally intended them to live which is the life of righteousness. Different people perform different tasks, yet all carry their Creator's genes and reflect something of who He is. Because we are living in the fallen state, God sent Jesus into the world to save all these souls. Through the life of Jesus, and the power of the Holy Spirit poured out to us through His wounded side, death, and resurrection, we correct the bad spiritual biology generated by sin and bring our soul back into conformity with the Sinless One. In other words, we try to get back to that untainted DNA which makes up the Christlike image. It's our soul that does this, but it's our soul that has to want it: has to call on God for mercy, for forgiveness, for enough grace to try to live the life of Christ.

What, therefore, is the soul's function? For this earthly life, the soul is God's most responsible agent in the development of sainthood from that which is fallen man. As the soul's unredeemed faculties are each brought into conformity to the law of love, the new man is formed from the old. Thus the soul which comprises these faculties is God's agent of transformation in man—it is the *embodiment* of the *process* of redemption. This process is activated only by the energy of love, and that love comes to each soul only through the free will of its possessor. As you call for love, respond to love, sacrifice to love, you empower your soul to effect your own transformation. Through your soul, you are co-creator with God of your unique image of Him.

What is the soul's relation to God and to the human body of flesh and blood? The relationship of the immortal soul to God is bonded in the sacrificial love and blood of Christ. It is a unique connection designed to confer upon believers an inheritance and portion of divine intelligence, goodness, virtue, glory, and a destiny expressly reserved for His kingdom of love comprised of many mansions and celestial spheres spoken of by Jesus, St. Paul, and St. John the Apostle. But it all begins here, on earth, in a body of unbridled and fallen human flesh. What, then, is the soul's relationship to the human body? The body is designed by God in Heaven as a vehicle for the soul. The external senses of the flesh—sight, smell, hearing, feeling, taste—permit the outside world access to the soul. Thus, life is experienced in interconnected dimensions: the external-physical linked with the internal-spiritual. What we perceive in our consciousness through our external and internal senses assists in the formation of knowledge about who and what we are, when we are and are not, from whence we came, to where we hope we will go: the pilgrimage of man's journey from the Genesis of Adam to the last step of the last person included in St. John's Revelation.

How we "will" to live—how we control our lives in conduct and behavior in our bodies—is the "filming action" of which I spoke: that chronicling which takes place in our souls. Failure to conduct ourselves with spiritual sobriety contributes to the soul's sickness within. When we sin, we cause a self-induced illness. Consider a widespread modern proof of how abuse of the body creates affliction of the soul. A person addicted to drugs or alcohol has no free will (a faculty of the soul). The appetites and desires rule and are rampant—without control. The emotions are placed into upheaval, the mind is stricken with anxiety and, inevitably, the heart grows troubled. Thus the soul in its entirety is led astray and corrupted. Worse still, out of desperation, the individual driven by this overpowering habit may resort to stealing, prostitution, and even murder; he or she is a slave overpowered by one of the soul's weakened faculties (appetites and desires) gone astray through the body's craving for a poisoned food. The human body, we are taught, is a living temple of the Holy Spirit. Practice moderation: proper care for your body will promote a healthy relationship with your soul.

In marriage, the harmony of spiritual unity within marital oneness is realized more easily when each spouse understands the importance and proper function of their soul. God blesses marriage with sanctified love so, when the two become one, the soul of that unity of love is joy unto Him and a reward of rich, unspeakable blessings to husband and wife.

Singleness of Heart

Most people, when using the word "heart," more or less mean it to be the vital center of one's being. Early rabbinical thinkers understood the heart as the "temple of the intellect" from whence the soul's faculties would receive their basic, first cause impulse or impression, moving a person to think or act. Solomon admonishes: "With all watchfulness keep thy heart, because life issueth out from it" (Prov 4:23). Centuries later in His Sermon on the Mount, our Lord Jesus taught the people where their treasure should be—not where moths can eat it nor rust corrupt it—saying: "For where thy treasure is, there is thy heart also" (Matt 6:21).

As the most intimate faculty of the soul, the heart plays an important role in man's conduct. Jesus explains: "...the things which come out from a man, they defile a man. For from within out of the heart of men proceed evil thoughts, adulteries, fornications, murders, thefts, covetousness, wickedness, deceit, lasciviousness, an evil eye, blasphemy, pride, foolishness. All these evil things come from within, and defile a man" (Mark 7:20-23).

The emanating center, the heart of man, must be kept

with all diligence: Christ preached this truth to humanity and, seven hundred years earlier, spoke it through His servant Solomon. A person may appear to be outwardly righteous while, within, spiritual corruption is consuming the soul as a raging fire feeds on dry grass to fuel its destructive course.

In marriage, singleness of heart begins when each spouse commits his or her heart to Him Who "triest the reins and hearts" (Jer 11:20) and then both spouses committing their hearts to maintaining the purity of their love to and for each other. Without this commitment, though we appear on the surface to be wholesome to each other, we have only concealed our inner defilement. Thus, the spiritual unity of marital oneness—the stability and peace in marriage—is being secretly undermined because singleness is not being genuinely forged and bonded in our interior life with unblemished love.

Marriage is a gift, a treasure of love. Therefore if husband and wife wish and pray for that gift to endure, that is where their hearts must be. As Jeremiah prophesies:

> Behold the days shall come, saith the Lord, and I will make a new covenant with the house of Israel, and with the house of Judah: Not according to the covenant which I made with their fathers, in the day that I took them by the hand to bring them out of the land of Egypt:

the covenant which they made void, and I had dominion over them, saith the Lord. But this shall be the covenant that I will make with the house of Israel, after those days, saith the Lord: I will give my law in their bowels, and I will write it in their heart: and I will be their God, and they shall be my people. (Jer 31:31-33)

Prayer

As Christ prays for and with His Bride, the Church, so too must you, as husband and wife, present yourselves in prayer before the Almighty Lord who joined you. However firmly a couple steers their marital conscience toward unity, differences of opinion will inevitably arise. Placing yourselves together in the presence of God in prayer and renouncing those things which hinder the marital relationship can only foster confidence in each other's intentions while balancing your interior lives with your exterior actions toward each other.

Pray to love each other in purity (without blemish) and sacredness (with dimensions of the divine). Should you desire to pray and your spouse refuse, exercise patience just as Christ patiently waits when you also are slow to turn to prayer. Seek God's effectual healing to remove whatever the obstacle may be in your spouse's reluctant attitude. Pray not for patience but for a loving patience.

The Jewish sages designated a specialty in prayer which they called "Kavanath Halev" meaning "direction of the heart": a worshipping of God by the heart. Psalm 51:6 teaches us that God loves sincerity of heart. Your prayers to God need to proceed from a sincere, authentic, non-pretending heart. Praying sincerely, you slowly starve vanity, pride, hypocrisy, and all the other subtle parasitic minions which emanate from spiritual immaturity and weaknesses. If your prayer is to have power, it must be honest in substance: you do not qualify or edit your prayer for the ear of your spouse. Spouses come before God as allies seeking power to deal with temptations and deceptions. Real concerns come out, and together, they determine courses of action to correct bad habits, double-mindedness, immaturity, and faulty emotions. Seeing each other act on these resolutions—working individually at marital unity—brings strength and depth to their love.

When you genuinely pray, you don't betray that prayer: verbal prayer is the most intimate sharing between husband, wife, and God which can foster trust and further growth in unity. By being truthful and sincere when praying together, you and your spouse enhance God's manifold glory in yourselves and in your common spiritual identity. Even when encountering the frustrating trials and complex temptations of daily life, His glory remains and sustains you if, holding it precious, you remain steadfast in truth and sincerity.

Therefore, pray together the same way you eat and drink together, laugh and cry together, play together, and most important of all, love together.

Grace

There are times in a marriage when only by God's grace can a husband and wife love each other. There are strains and pressures which enter marriage because of the sin, weakness, pride, and faults of the two imperfect human beings involved. These pressures and weaknesses may dangerously compound: a fault in one spouse can play on the mind and spirit of the other, causing even innocent words, actions, or motives to be misconstrued. In the midst of anger, hurt, and disappointment, each spouse may blame the whole problem on the weaknesses of the other. For persons developing in the role of husband or wife, how they face and deal with human frailties—their own and their partner's—will make or break their union.

Rather than being overwhelmed at the moment of emotional distress because of disappointment and clouded reasoning, seek God's grace to deal with and lead you through the situation. Your distress can, with God's help, evolve into a desire for enrichment to overcome the despair at hand. "I am the vine: you the branches: he that abideth in me, and I in him, the same beareth much fruit: for without me you can do nothing" (John 15:5). "For it is God who worketh in you, both to will and to accomplish, according to his good will" (Phil 2:13). "Or what hast thou that thou hast not received?" (1 Cor 4:7). It is certain then that God's grace is given to us by God's express desire to help us achieve a balanced handling of our "will" in order to do the right thing in life.

Let us be mindful, then—as we, in our hurt and confusion, come to what falsely appears to be an end to our efforts—that Jesus never gives up on His Bride, the Church. In charity let us look for solutions and, in so doing, we can be enriched and healed by His grace. Marriage with all its practical problems is also the image of the miracle of miracles, Christ saving His Bride, the Church. The latter happens because of God's grace and love; likewise, within you and your spouse there exists, by His will and blessings, the grace for you to experience your own personal, private, and intimate miracle of evolving and everlasting unity.

Devotion

In Ephesians, St. Paul states: "For we are his workmanship, created in Christ Jesus in good works, which God hath prepared that we should walk in them" (Eph 2:10). Recognizing then that this is our heritage, that we are the result of His workmanship, how do we help in the day-to-day process of being formed into the artwork of God? We can do this by cultivating the values of devotion.

Devotion is a deeper, more practiced attentiveness to spiritual things. It embraces spiritually understood knowledge about God, prayer, love, and heartfelt imitation of Him in His love towards us. It is a more intense affection: the commitment of wanting to be a little bit better in the eyes of God. Devotion involves a prayerful life growing in the dimensions of an atmosphere filled with God's spirit and creative forces of love. As His handiwork, we draw life from Him. And, as in Genesis, life is infused into us by His breath, the Holy Spirit. Prayer is more necessary to the soul than water is to the body: water passes through the body and out into the drain whereas prayer leaves your heart and remains forever in the bosom and love of God.

As human souls, we are capable of reflecting on ourselves with spiritual self-cognition: reexamining life as we have lived it, whether squandered in sin or improved in God's truth and perfect liberty. Since we are an imperishable image of Him, we are ordained in this present life of human suffering to a glorious future. We are united to God by bonds of willful surrender to His mercy and forgiveness and therefore are devoted to Him for life. By abusing our liberty, we render impotent the providential plan that He set in motion from the beginning.

We must forsake whatever hinders our union with God, which is a gradual transition like the coming of dawn from darkness. Our spiritual misdeeds spawn spiritual ills which demand a slow cure. We must be patient while we are cleansed: in our devotion to Him, we must keep our hearts loyal in both pleasure and pain, plenty and want. Remember, "Know ye that the Lord he is God: he made us, and not we ourselves. We are his people and the sheep of his pasture" (Ps 99:3).[2]

In marriage, devotion to God catalyzes His power to form in the two of you the unfathomable, impossible miracle of oneness. Through devotion to Him, husband and wife gradually break the bonds of self-serving sin. They must seek His help for the sins which beset their marital conscience. They must renounce them with sorrow. There must be repentance and amendment when seeking forgiveness.

---

[2] In the Latin Vulgate and the Douay-Rheims, this Psalm is numbered 99. In more recent translations, this Psalm is numbered 100.

In *The Imitation of Christ*, Thomas à Kempis reflects on confession of sin:

> You are the soul's sweet refreshment; the man who receives you worthily will share by inheritance the everlasting glory. But how often I slip into sin; how quickly I grow dull of heart and neglectful! That is why it is vital for me to freshen myself, to clean myself, to stir the fire in my heart by frequent prayer and confession. If I neglect these means too long, I may fall away from my good resolutions.

One cannot sin and not repent without being hurt. Our hearts must free themselves from sin's noxious attachment. Devotion to God with an unburdened conscience makes it easier for us to live and breathe the spiritual life He meant us to have. It also enables love to flow unobstructed between husband and wife, promoting the deeper, mystical union for which they long and which has its highest expression in Christ's union with His Bride, the Church.

God never tires of asking us to change our ways so He can share more of His love, everlasting joy, and glory with us. Therefore, pray together and resolve to abandon ingratitude and disloyalty toward each other and whatever manifestations of vanity encumber husband and/or wife. Ask that you be delivered from the attachment to useless and perilous thoughts and actions. Be kind to each other's wishes and listen thoughtfully to the issues and concerns inhabiting each other's hearts. We all have imperfections which tend to foster evil inclinations within us. Pray to be preserved and guarded while waiting patiently for His spiritual gifts and fruits to nourish the miracle of a mystical joy in marriage.

A marriage without devotion to higher and more noble causes will wallow in the surface values of a shallow, rootless, and thoughtless love. Devote yourselves to a devout marriage. Love one another fervently in Christ.

Communication

It is important in marriage that truth spoken in love be the basis from which thoughts are transmitted. Some of our ancient Jewish cousins, the Talmudic scholars, held fast to the belief that the faculty of speech was a gift which only God could give to man. This is supportable because, on the sixth day of creation, sacred scripture states: "And God created man to his own image: to the image of God he created him: male and female he created them. And God blessed them, *saying*..." (Gen 1:27-28).

God created man in His own image and likeness: the creator *spoke* to His creatures by *saying* to them...and they spoke to Him. By pronouncing the blessing upon our first earthly father and mother, God conferred upon them the gift and power of understanding and speech.

When using this gift of speech, therefore, be mindful that it is a powerful faculty—so powerful in fact that our Lord raised the dead with His voice. He also commanded demons to flee from the suffering souls in His presence. He ordered the winds and waves to be still, and they obeyed. Truth in speech is so powerful it can penetrate the darkest minds or reach and set free the innermost depths of a soul enslaved by the bonds of heinous sins.

Listed among the six things which the Lord hates, Solomon's Proverbs mentions "a lying tongue" (Prov 6:17). Further on it is written, "The lip of truth shall be steadfast for ever: but he that is a hasty witness, frameth a lying tongue....Lying lips are an abomination to the Lord: but they that deal faithfully please him" (Prov 12:19, 22). Lying is an intentional abuse of language. It violates, distorts, and harms the natural order of truth. Most importantly, it robs man of his dignity and undermines the noble station upon which he is to stand when speaking of truths concerning the image and likeness of God. Jesus warns us that the unbelieving Jews of His time could not believe Him because they could not understand His language. They could not understand Him or the truths He spoke because their hearts were hardened—deafened and deadened—by living a life made up of lies. They hear and heed a different master. Jesus tells them:

> Why do you not know my speech?
> Because you cannot hear my word.
> You are of your father the devil,
> and the desires of your father you will do....
> When he speaketh a lie,
> he speaketh of his own:
> for he is a liar, and the father thereof (John 8:43-44).

By lying to each other, husband and wife injure the confidence and trust which binds their love together. Sometimes we can invite Satan into our heart quite knowingly, thereby ushering the father of lies and his minions into our hearts, desecrating the gift of speech and weakening our ability to communicate in love, beauty, and with meaningful purpose. Lies destabilize the delicate marital unity of oneness and fracture the solidarity of marriage. When speaking of the new life in Christ, St. Paul admonishes the Ephesians by saying, "Wherefore putting away lying, speak ye the truth every man with his neighbour; for we are members one of another" (Eph 4:25).

In marriage, you are given to each other in the most intimate way so that two people, by God's command, can unite and become one. Love and respect each other's dignity by speaking and building each other up in the truth. Although it may be painful at times because of unpleasant emotions, truth heals: it dispels darkness and corrects unbelief. "He that speaketh that which he knoweth, sheweth forth justice" (Prov 12:17). To show forth justice in marriage involves committing yourselves to fairness in issues that could be emotionally explosive: to treat your spouse fairly as you expect your spouse to treat you. Showing forth justice means a constructive and positive focusing of truth in order to build a vision—the opposite of purposefully clouding or disguising an issue. Living a life of truth develops and sustains a pure conscience. Loving the truth fosters good spiritual health within marriage. Seeking the truth leads the soul to an atmosphere devoid of guilt in which peace becomes the gravity anchoring the heart amidst times of emotional unrest or conflict. Communicate to each other as Christ communicates with you and the rest of creation: truthfully.

Change

"If then any be in Christ a new creature, the old things are passed away, behold all things are made new. But all things are of God..." (2 Cor 5:17-18).

The process of redemption is an ongoing movement and progression from the fallen state to the resurrected mode of being "a new creature." In marriage, the changes inevitably affecting spouses can be an unnerving experience eroding whatever composure may have been present under previous circumstances. In the non-committed Christian marital experience, this composure often derives from deep-rooted attitudes, values, or priorities to which the couple unconsciously adhere: a sort of marital "automatic pilot" which dictates the direction of marriage. Yet when change disrupts that composure and a couple recognizes their marriage as unfulfilling and bankrupt, the decision to make another try demands spouses take inventory to consciously, actively salvage whatever is enriching their unity and discard that which is destroying it.

Change is inevitable and constant. As the personal shedding process continues and "the new creature" emerges—takes substance—from the old, it is important for spouses in their trials and struggles to communicate the "whys" of their decisions for change. Husband and wife are two distinct, separate human beings. Each has a unique personality and, therefore, each must experience the character transformation process in a specific and individual way. Yet they are involved in a single movement with a single goal: the marital unity of two becoming one. This common vision they must never forget.

In a marriage actively committed to the Lordship of Christ, each spouse will need to consciously undergo change focused on outgrowing old, unredeemed habits of behavior which are not only disruptive to marital unity but also corruptive to the faculties of the soul. The Christian values each spouse exhibits at home in the presence of the other or in front of children must not be dropped at the door when he or she leaves for work. The process of transformation gently requires that we as spouses live our values wherever we may be, not betray each other and Christ by turning those values off and on according to whim or desire. To alter one's attitude or reshape one's values when in the presence of someone other than your spouse is to conceal the Face of the new creature with a mask of hypocrisy. The tender seedling of truth, just gaining strength within, is willfully stifled—suppressed—beneath the hardened social games people have been playing for centuries and centuries. These games are never new; the players are.

Patience exercised from the heart is the essential virtue when a Christian couple makes the commitment to consciously seek God-given love in and for each other: patience to embrace and work through the unsettling changes God requires of those who choose to be reborn together. Time must be set aside for prayerful discussions on the issues of change: reevaluating the priorities at work within the marriage such as the Jones versus Jones consumer mind-set and the degree of materialistic drive for "necessities"; taking a hard look together at unexamined behaviors such as social drinking habits and socially acceptable flirtation overtures that suggest "it's okay to look and tease but not to touch"; and other issues, unique to each couple.

Changes in marriage must begin in the heart, proceeding out into the faculties of the soul and witnessed in the multicolors of personality as well as the pillared foundation of character.

Millenniums ago, the prophet Ezekiel spoke to Israel about the remnant to be saved; his words are a beacon and promise to committed Christian couples today: "And I will give them one heart, and will put a new spirit in their bowels: and I will take away the stony heart out of their flesh, and will give them a heart of flesh: That they may walk in my commandments, and keep my judgments, and do them: and that they may be my people, and I may be their God" (Ezek 11:19-20).

Peace and Tranquility

> Submit thyself then to him, and be at peace:
> > and thereby thou shalt have the best fruits.
> Receive the law of his mouth,
> > and lay up his words in thy heart.
> If thou wilt return to the Almighty,
> > thou shalt be built up,
> and shalt put away iniquity
> > far from thy tabernacle....
> Then shalt thou abound in delights in the Almighty,
> > and shalt lift up thy face to God.
> Thou shalt pray to him, and he will hear thee,
> > and thou shalt pay vows....
> and light shall shine in thy ways (Job 22.21-23, 26-28).

Make peace with Him. Be reconciled to Him in and through Christ. Confess your sins to God; do penance, and bring forth fruits worthy of repentance. Accept His mercy with earnestness and calm joy, believing in your heart that Christ died for your sins.

Make peace with your spouse. Be reconciled, and your happiness in your marriage will be restored. The light of His love will shine in your marital oneness, and your singleness of heart will fill your journey with blessings and joy along His path.

How often in the mad push and rush of modern life do we stop to take recourse within ourselves? Perhaps we so infrequently retire into our own souls because we are poor inside: there is a poverty of Christ-like virtue and values; we cannot find true peace because the thoughts we are looking at are so poor. Scripture gives us this interior wealth: spiritually potent riches of wisdom and revelation which can sustain our contemplations and inward retreats come to us when the mad push and rush of demands are put in their proper place. Peace from Christ is always there when we surrender to the presence of carrying our personal crosses.

Jesus tells us it is necessary to pick up our daily cross; though it may be painful at times, those pains will produce the fruits of peace because that is what God promises will happen in obedient surrender to His will.

"Peace I leave with you, my peace I give unto you: not as the world giveth, do I give unto you" (John 14:27).

"Come to me, all you that labour, and are burdened, and I will refresh you. Take up my yoke upon you, and learn of me, because I am meek, and humble of heart: *and you shall find rest to your souls.* For my yoke is sweet and my burden light" (Matt 11:28-30).

"And the work of justice shall be peace, and the service of justice quietness, and security for ever. And my people shall sit in the beauty of peace, and in the tabernacles of confidence, and in wealthy rest" (Isa 32:17-18).

"Much peace have they that love thy law, and to them there is no stumbling block" (Ps 118:165).[3]

"Now the Lord of peace himself give you everlasting peace in every place" (2 Thess 3:16).

These scriptures promise us that peace for our souls is a *gift*. Interior tranquility is the result of a process which begins in our daily, momentary reconciliation to God and reaches fruition only as the faculties of our souls become spiritually aligned with the order and disposition of the Giver.

Therefore, retire into your souls with His Light: contemplate His laws and eternal principles of love, purity, and fidelity. Pray with your spouse, asking peace upon your marriage. Just as a seedling cannot grow to perfection of its beauty if unprotected amidst the conflicting elements of raging storms, so your marriage must be fenced about with peace amidst the subtle temptations, wearing pressures, and spiritual turmoil brought to bear upon it.

Remember it is the Lord of peace who gives peace—and also remember that tranquility is never independent of your free will. Christ Himself willed this for us when He said: "Peace I leave with you, my peace I give unto you: not as the world giveth, do I give unto you. Let not your heart be

---

[3] In the Latin Vulgate and the Douay-Rheims, this Psalm is numbered 118. In more recent translations, this Psalm is numbered 119.

troubled, nor let it be afraid" (John 14:27). Desire His offer always and will it in your lives because it is God who wills and fulfills His promises in you. Seek peace in your marriage. It is the gentle gravity of love.

Trust

Can the Church, the Bride of Christ, trust her Lord? Most assuredly! What is Christian trust? It is when you hope with divine confidence. It is a sense leading to a virtuous belief. Can you barely trust your spouse? Or is trust something possessed and exercised by both of you as a sacred dimension essential to the bonding of your relationship?

Do you trust the Lord for your salvation? Do you trust the pilot flying the jetliner to your destination? Do you trust your spouse? yourself? Those whom you trust have proven disciplines which make them the trusted people they are. Christ proved His lordship, overcoming sin and death by being raised from the dead. Why can He alone offer humankind this proof? Because He alone walked this earth in perfect adherence and humble obedience to the Father's Will. Dependable airline pilots are faithful in adhering to the professional disciplines and observing the laws which keep an aircraft aloft and on-course. In the same way, spouses can trust each other only as they become aware of and adhere to the laws which govern the creation and nurturing of spiritual unity. Unless these laws are understood and practiced, strains, stresses, and sin will fracture trust and "put asunder" what God has joined together.

And we need to trust. Christian trust is sacred ointment: it mystically binds marital elements with the energizing and healing powers of love. It brings longevity to a relationship because it is a friend and close companion to long-suffering. It gives latitude for growth. Trusting means letting go of some of your concerns for your spouse, permitting each to directly approach God without unnecessary interference from the other while learning to develop his or her own powers of decision. Thus Christian trust is a gateway through which other graces enter and assist God with the perfecting of your spouse's virtue and character—a gateway each spouse opens for the other.

Marital trust also involves the active recognition that our individual vision is limited—that we must express our perceptions/opinions honestly in the way that we understand them and then trust that dynamic, mystical interaction of God, spouse, and ourselves to bring us eventually to a completed, *multi-dimensional* understanding. In this way, trust goes hand-in-hand with patience. We suffer our own limits of vision as much as we suffer our spouse's imperfections. Together, as husband and wife, we trust God to use our limitations and imperfections to help us create each other into His complete vision of who we are in Christ.

How is Christian trust established? It begins in the spirit

of sincere prayer. It is when both husband and wife kneel before the Almighty Creator and bare their hearts in devotion to Him that the sacredness of those moments seed the heart with trust.

Fear

> I sought the Lord, and he heard me;
> and he delivered me from all my troubles.
> Come ye to him and be enlightened:
> and your faces shall not be confounded. (Ps 33.5-6)[4]

There are times when a combination of circumstances—anxiety, uncertainty, guilt, or imbalanced perspectives—cause fear to become the prevailing miserable weather of the soul. When doubting one's ability, success, or spirituality, the feeling of uncertainty will lead the individual on to bare the diminishing sensibilities of his or her soul to taunting, shadowy perceptions that mislead the mind, sending the person's reason anxiously pacing onto the path of confusion.

As Christians, it is a God-given responsibility for us to take inventory of our abilities, successes/failures, and depth of spirituality. However, this self-evaluation should be done in an atmosphere of a conscious trust of God's ability to lovingly accomplish His intentions for our souls rather than the

---

[4] In the Latin Vulgate and the Douay-Rheims, these verses are numbered as verses 5-6 of Psalm 33. In more recent translations, these verses are numbered as verses 4-5 of Psalm 34.

darkened suggestions of an uncertain mind led astray by suspicious fears.

One of the most effective counter-offensives to soul-harassing fears is to develop and maintain spiritual disciplines with a pure and educated faith in Christ, "the author and finisher of faith" (Heb 12:2). These disciplines should involve praying daily, reading scripture that records how God saves His people, and attending worship services in a sincere spirit with a humble heart. Confess your sins to God, and ask pardon of those you offend. Be genuine in your dealings with man and God: shun hypocrisy. Do not avoid or neglect doing whatever good you can for the Body of Christ and others who do not know Him as the Saviour of man.

Fear afflicts all human beings. For those who are immature in the spirit, there is no need to despair. Being inexperienced in the spirit is a natural process leading into maturity: adversity is a healthy opportunity for growth, development, and success. St. Paul's epistle to Timothy is a classic example to all of us who are young in the spirit and in need of encouragement and strengthening. The young Timothy must at times have been overwhelmed as he was instructed in the many areas of responsibility concerning duties and qualifications of different church officers. Further, he was pastorally counseled by St. Paul on his own duties and obligations as a "man of God." St. Paul advises Timothy: "For which cause I admonish thee, that thou stir up the grace of God which is in thee, by the imposition of my hands. For God hath not given us the spirit of fear: but of power, and of love, and of sobriety" (2 Tim 1:6-7).

Should you or your spouse experience extended periods of fear of whatever sorts, be they spiritual, ill health, financial, or from another cause, retreat calmly into prayer and study the many examples recorded for us in the Salvation History of God saving His people. Cherish the thought that God has not given us "the spirit of fear: but of power, and of love, and of sobriety." Remember that as co-heir with Christ, and having a humbled heart, grace is always available: the transforming power of God's love is ever-present to redeem that which is afraid, confused, and lost, by placing these within the sphere of His all-embracing care, His Mercy. It is an abundance of gifts.

> For I know the thoughts that I think towards you, saith the Lord, thoughts of peace, and not of affliction, to give you an end and patience. And you shall call upon me, and you shall go: and you shall pray to me, and I will hear you. You shall seek me, and shall find me: when you shall seek me with all your heart. And I will be found by you, saith the Lord.... (Jer 29:11-14)

There is good reason to fear Yahweh whom we only come to know personally in Jesus Christ. When a person has a deeply committed reverence for God, realizing His great power and love for man, obedience becomes our way of life. The respect and awe is so desperately needed for us to accommodate God's great, pure, and holy love in our tiny struggling and developing human hearts. And it is in this great and holy love that we painfully grow and respond to God.

Too many of us are unsure about God's love in our lives. We are unsure of His support for us in our trials, be they health issues, loss of employment, finances, the loss of loved ones, and the list goes on. Without a healthy fear of God, how are we going to manage with life's issues that usher fear into our lives?

We are God's children baptized into the Body of Christ. As such we should meet those fears with the holy fear of God—knowing because we are in Him, He is with us. As Catholics, we know—as St. Paul preaches—that we do, and will, suffer in and through those trials which assail us.

> The fear of the Lord is the beginning of wisdom:
> and the knowledge of the holy is prudence.
> For by me shall thy days be multiplied,
> and years of life shall be added to thee.
> If thou be wise, thou shalt be so to thyself:
> and if a scorner, thou alone shalt bear the evil. (Prov 9:10-12)

Having a humble fear of God and His love will allow us, in

His mercy, to live through fear-without-reason, which sometimes floods and darkens our minds and delivers us into a near paralysis. God loves us in that very moment through the pain and suffering. God delivers individuals. Are you wise enough in your love for Him to trust that Jesus is always with you, not only covering us with His blanket of love, but also within your pain and suffering. Don't ever forget: "For the spirit of the Lord hath filled the whole world: and that, which containeth all things, hath knowledge of the voice" (Wis 1:7).

Pray to Him. Talk to Him. Trust that He hears you and rest, knowing that He hears you and is with you, in you, and through you. He knows you! Pray to know Him.

Vision

When prophecy shall fail, the people shall be scattered abroad:
but he that keepeth the law is blessed. (Prov 29:18)

Now ask yourselves: Does Christ have a vision for the marriage to His Bride, the Church? The answer is an obvious yes! Another question you must ask yourselves: Do I have a vision for my marriage? If your answer is no, there exists the probability of its being injured and even perishing.

What goes into or makes up a vision for marriage? Love, faithfulness, fidelity, care and concern, patience, mercy, long-suffering, humility, pragmatism, unity, and joy. One of Christ's chief characteristics in His marriage to the Church is the quality of His redeeming love and power. Correspondingly, you must allow Christ to imbue your marriage with His love and power if you are to attain and sustain the virtues necessary to your marital vision. The power of the Holy Spirit given to you at baptism, the results of sincere prayer, the frequent receiving of the Holy Eucharist, and every effort made to maintain the life of grace: all these are the spiritual avenues by which the marital vision is strengthened, enriched, and made holy.

Also contributing to the sustaining and growth of the marital vision is the practice of down-to-earth pragmatism, shared and discussed together. The author of our faith, Jesus Christ, admonishes us on the values of reason when He states:

> For which of you having a mind to build a tower, doth not first sit down, and reckon the charges that are necessary, whether he have wherewithal to finish it?...Or what king, about to go to make war against another king, doth not first sit down, and think whether he be able, with ten thousand, to meet him that, with twenty thousand, cometh against him? (Luke 14:28, 31)

Christ is emphasizing the use and importance of calculated considerations. It is important to be thankful that God is the author of both reason and faith. These are balanced and complementary instruments used to assist us in our understanding, growth, and development.

When questioning our Lord on the placement of "reason" in my life, the Spirit led me into the forest to observe this question:

> *Behold the spider weaving its web. Do you think it will ever entangle itself with the life which it weaves?*

"No," I replied.

Then why in life does man entangle and injure himself with the life which he weaves?

Giving this question careful thought while observing the spider for hours busily at work, I said to the Lord:

"Unlike the sinfully blind who lead the spiritually blind and both fall into the ditch, the spider lives by the spirit which came into him at birth and is not blinded by willful sin to Your Will and Spirit in his heart. And so he weaves with Your Spirit the will for his life, and thus he is sheltered, protected, and fed."

And so be faithful and humble to the predestined laws and spirit of matrimony. The unity in marriage is set and determined by God's plan, gifts, and standards. Share your concerns with each other and give careful consideration to the requirements which must be met and dealt with. Contribute to the single vision which love offers a couple joined in oneness. Be flexible in the direction of your journey with marital love, but also firm in your conviction that the steps which you take together be pious in thought and pragmatic in action.

Such vision implies a sensing of something not quite present or visible to the eye. It is a stirring of the mind, the heart. It refers to an anticipation because of a divinely inspired concept. Vision in marriage requires sacrifice. Both you and your spouse must yield to humility when love corrects and adjusts the direction of your journey enroute to your marital vision. A balanced marriage requires a singular, synoptic vision utilizing two hearts, minds, wills, strengths, and emotional cooperation. This vision can only come about and mature in its mystical focus when two beings in matrimony are united in the purity of each other's love and respect. Remember, most important of all, vision results from the forces of charity busily at work. Therefore, be charitable with one another as Christ is charitable with His Bride, the Church.

Faith and Reason

Life is a process of problem-solving. As Christian spouses make their day-to-day journey together, they may look at the problems they encounter through the spiritual eye of "faith," which operates according to God's practicalities, and/or the rational, reasonable, practical eye of "reason," which operates according to the world's practicalities. Serious marital rifts occur if spouses do not understand the wise application of these perspectives to a particular problem and/or do not recognize through which "eye" each of them is evaluating and making a decision about the issue. Always remember that reason is not in opposition to faith; rather, faith is the culmination of reason.

What is the spiritual perspective which can be termed "faith"? What is the practical, rational perspective which can be termed "reason"? Contemplating these questions in the youth of my Christian walk—and failing to arrive at any satisfying answers—I took them with me one day into the dense forests of the mountains. "Lord," I prayed, "teach me about faith and reason." This is what I learned: faith and reason are like two trees. Although similar in appearance, their inner natures are significantly different. This disparity is not apparent when the weather is fair, the soil moist, the sun gently shining: the two bask in peace and together grow happily in the nourishing warmth of the day.

However, when seeing the darkness of an approaching storm, the tree called "Reason"—lacking faith—fears for her life and worries about what the winds will do to her branches and beautiful leaves. Meanwhile, the tree called "Faith," seeing the same violent storm approaching, tells herself, "I will gather my life down within the depths of my roots and bend my branches with the gales of the wind. My leaves I will sacrifice to the hunger of the tempest and soil—and in the peace of Him who planted me here, I will await the passing of the storm."

Limited human "Reason" may fear and suffer for the loss of the day, while "Faith" blesses the name of her God knowing that, apart from the day, she has life for tomorrow. While human "Reasoning" takes her joy from shallow knowledge of the transient life (she sees only in her *leaves*), "Faith" keeps her joy in the knowledge that within the depths of her *roots,* as well as the soil she has fed with her sacrifices, are leaves yet to be born: she finds her peace in the certitude of life being made anew.

Human beings—including Christian spouses—are like these two trees of Reason and Faith. In good "spiritual weather," our appearances are similar but, when conflicting elements assault us, the varying perspectives of our inner natures are revealed. We respond differently to the storms of life, tending to look at a problem with the eye of faith or with the eye of practicality. What we need to understand is that each perspective can provide a dimension of wisdom to the other. The eye of rational practicality tempers the perspective of faith. Yet, as Christian couples, the eye of faith is our root: that to which, like the tree of "Faith," we take recourse during the storm and in which we find our treasure and stronghold. The marital relationship is spiritual and, therefore, the eye of faith should be our fundamental reality. If necessary, we are correct to sacrifice the temporal in order to preserve the eternal.

As Christian spouses, we should not be threatened by a disparity in perspectives, but rather use those differences to reach a wiser solution. Instead of resorting to anger, impatience, or bitterness, we must clarify to each other our perceptions and understandings of an issue—the "eye" we each are using—truly listening with open hearts and taking time to discuss the various ways of evaluating our problem. We need to listen. And we must not neglect to pray together for a wise application of practical/faithful perspectives to the problem at hand.

Do not forget that it is God who created both our rational and our spiritual mind: it is given to us to understand both "what is seen and what is unseen." Reason is a natural gift, the means by which we think and are taught to be practical. Faith is supernatural, a virtue whereby we believe and learn from Him who is our Root, Image, and God. Both perspectives are necessary if we are to meet the continuous challenges and difficulties of life with effective wisdom and ultimate success.

Human Sexuality

It is an ancient mystery. It is an experience steeped in the intense sensations of its senses throughout the body's flesh as well as its soul. In human sexuality there is a certain transforming life force impacting the spiritual faculties of the soul—the heart with its emotions, free will, intellect with its memory and imagination, and the appetites and desires. Consequently, the penalty of extra-marital sex prevents some people from inheriting the Kingdom of God.

> ...but the body is not for fornication, but for the Lord, and the Lord for the body.... Know you not that your bodies are the members of Christ? Shall I then take the members of Christ, and make them the members of an harlot? God forbid. Or know you not, that he who is joined to a harlot, is made one body? For they shall be, saith he, *two in one flesh*.... Fly fornication. Every sin that a man doth, is without the body; but he that committeth fornication, sinneth against his own body. (1 Cor 6:13b, 15-16, 18)

We are advised and cautioned against immoral sexual actions by St. Paul. We are called back from the ancientness of sin's corruption to a new sexual wholesomeness and a sacred marital unity in Christ, sanctified, within the Body of the faithful, to which no prostitutional or promiscuous act can be a part.

Sex is mysteriously powerful. It can be both a dark and light-filled mystery, a phenomenon; its complexity of experiences ruptures any single attempt at a complete definition of what it is. It is powerful and can be spiritually deadening to the faculties of the soul, so that the Apostle tells us these sorts of people "will never inherit the kingdom of God," which Jesus tells us, in all four Gospels, is already here, but there are preconditions for entering.

Sexual immorality has a dark history. God cautions us. So do the prophets. In Matthew 5:28, Jesus talks to us about committing adultery in our hearts. The Apostle Paul warns us in Ephesians 5:5, Romans 1:29+, Galatians 5:21, Ephesians 2:1-6, and Titus 3:3-7. The Apostle Peter tells us people like this are joining a "confusion of riotousness" (1 Pet 4:4). Illicit sex can lead a person into a dark, eternal, and painful misery.

So much for the dark side of sinful sex. In the Book of Genesis, Abraham is entertaining three men with food which he had prepared. While waiting on them, they asked for Sarah.

"He answered: Lo, she is in the tent. And he

said to him: I will return and come to thee at this time, life accompanying, and Sara, thy wife, shall have a son. Which when Sara heard, she laughed behind the door of the tent. Now they were both old, and far advanced in years, and it had ceased to be with Sara after the manner of women. And she laughed secretly, saying: After I am grown old and my lord is an old man, shall I give myself to pleasure?" (Gen 18:9-12)

Sarah is saying "After I am grown old..., shall I give myself to pleasure?" Are we to understand that Sarah enjoyed the pleasures of her earlier sexual experiences? I think there is truth in the answer being yes. Since the birth of the Church and down through the ages and throughout the history of the Saints, we are wisely cautioned on sexual conduct. We need to be humble and not obstruct the wisdom which preceded us to warn and protect us from the power of sin in the sexual experience.

God is the Creator and Author, whose whole workmanship created our bodies and their abilities for sexual experiences including the holy fact that our bodies are also His temple. "Know you not, that you are the temple of God, and that the Spirit of God dwelleth in you? But if any man violate the temple of God, him shall God destroy. For the temple of God is holy, which you are" (1 Cor 3:16-17).

Do Christian couples stop having sex knowing they are temples of God? Obviously no. We would be a church without Prophets to lead us, Priests to celebrate the Holy Mass, Holy Orders without brothers and sisters to work in our hospitals and schools, Saints whose lives reflect the glory and presence of Christ, and Martyrs bearing the ultimate witness. In being born anew in the Spirit, our faith enables us to better understand this God-given gift and mystery with a vivid spiritual clarity and appreciation for the depths in which lawful pleasures innocently enrapture the senses without staining or harming one's soul. It allows us to enter the Kingdom as sexually active, joyful, and dynamic Christians whose fear of God sets us free from wrongful sex. Protect the inherent sanctity of your sexuality and God will allow the preordained joyful mystery of sex to freely unfold in its intended innocence.

In closing, let us be mindful of what the fourth century desert father—whom Thomas Merton quoted in his book, *The Wisdom of the Desert*—had to say about being chaste or a fornicator: "An elder said: Do not judge a fornicator if you are chaste, for if you do, you too are violating the law as much as he is. For He who said thou shall not fornicate also said thou shall not judge." Sex is obviously God's Creation. It is His sacred Mystery in its intended human innocence within creation. Live your sexual lives in His peaceful wisdom, and stand with your interior senses nakedly humbled and joyful before your loving and wise God.

The Marriage Bed

Sexual intercourse is God's idea! Intended to be a lawful, life-giving delight explored within marriage, sexual intimacy is exquisitely designed by Him to be a mystical yet tangible expression of love between spouses. Far from being a "utility" merely for the perpetuation of the human race, the sexual act provides endless imaginative, mystic, and pleasurable dimensions for husband and wife to discover, experience, and enjoy.

God's requirement that we keep the sexual act within marriage is not a restriction but a key: the Designer is opening to us the only door which will allow us to plumb and experience the full depths of our sexual natures and the profoundest possibilities of the sexual union. Marriage is that sacredly advised door. Keep in mind that when we die and go before our merciful God in judgment, we appear as a man/woman, husband/wife, father or mother. Our marriage bed is a sacred experience which will be judged in the intentions of the heart of our love. The Catechism of the Catholic Church has its teachings on the subject of Human Sexuality and its complex experiences. Also, an understanding of Pope John Paul II's

Theology of the Body will be a blessing to our growth in love. We will not be judged on how well we remembered what was taught. Rather, we will be judged on the intentions of our hearts, which only God's eyes can see.

Taking into consideration that life is a gift, God's Spirit is a gift unto the spirit of mankind. The spirit of God always offers direction to humanity. As such, sexual intercourse with all of its complexities, pleasures, dysfunctions, appetites and desires, and frustrations, in fallen human nature, needs guidance from the spirit of God. Man's spirit after being guided by the spirit of God needs to know what the requirements are for properly offering one's complete self to his/her spouse. Sexual intercourse is an offering of total self which includes the physical, emotional, and spiritual. Are spouses in and of themselves, excluding the guidance of God's spirit, capable of attaining a completely genuine physical, emotional, and spiritual union in purity of heart? I don't think so. Being perfectly married—physically, emotionally, and spiritually—is an exquisite and delicate lifetime multidimensional process requiring the spirit of God continuously assisting the growing faith in the lives of his children.

If we "would love" and truly experience the profound meanings of sexual union—the elusive paradisiacal fulfillment the secular world is continuously chasing and never possessing—it is necessary to follow the Designer's rules: "Marriage [is] honourable in all, and the bed undefiled. For fornicators and adulterers God will judge" (Heb 13:4). In a Christian union, the intentions of the sexual act must be kept pure. The simple rule is: *Be respectful of your spouse.* The quest for sensory fulfillment is a reciprocal delight in which husband and wife have distinctive and equal sexual needs to be met. Spouses must moderate, nurture, shape and reshape their sexual appetites relative to the needs and sexual personality of their wife or husband. Spouses must be sensitive to one another, tempering or stimulating their appetites to complement their spouse's—each shaping his/her individual sexual personality to create together a mystic reciprocity and a single, unique sexual identity of two complete and whole human-beings who blend spiritually into *one.*

Therefore, fence your marriage bed around with purity—both of thought and action: free your hearts from low principles and bad habits. For example, avoid immoderate desire: pray not to intoxicate yourself with sexual pleasures to the point of spiritual disorder and drunkenness. Fulfillment can be attained without the disgust of satiety. Further, avoid fornication and all forms of licentiousness. There is much affliction and sorrow in a soul whose memory contains sexual impurities. How can a husband or wife share intimately profound physical delights when their memories are filled with dark shapes and murmurings of other sexual activities, vain love, and forbidden pleasures, including social flirtations. If such shadows sicken your lawful intercourse, only through earnest repentance and purifying forgiveness can your memory be cleansed and set free.

Third, shun the act of masturbation—which is a fallen satisfaction fruited by concupiscence. Masturbation springs from self-love and spawns only self-concupiscence. In its haste for personal gratification and self-created fulfillment, this inordinate appetite robs a man or woman of a sanctified desire for the beloved. A specious "union" with self gradually saps—bleeds—the healthy, mystical hunger for physical, emotional, spiritual, and soulful unity with a spouse. Habitual masturbation increasingly chains the appetites and desires, imagination and memory, redirecting these from their proper, life-giving encounter—a spouse—back towards the self and destructive self-enslavement. Spiritually, masturbation is darkly potent; resist its falsely "gentle" temptations.

Masturbation is fornication through a different template. It is a different form through a deceptive sense. It is a pseudo-copulation whose misguided sexual exertions traverses one's soul into a realm of unreal reality—a virtual reality of virtual-species sex utilizing a single body and soul. It is a single person attempting a sexual act through two imagined people, involving a single soul. It is sexual misconduct against the body, spirit, and soul and its faculties as previously described by St. John of the Cross. "Or know you not, that your members are the temple of the Holy Ghost, who is in you, whom you have from God; and you are not your own? For you are bought with a great price. Glorify and bear God in your body" (1 Cor 6:19-20). *You have been bought and paid for.*

The powerful ancient mystery of evil transcends the individual's weakened ability to understand its complex role in the fundamental realities of appetites, desires, and lusts. For those who share the heritage and faith of our wise ancestor, Jesus Ben Sirach (132 B.C.):

> To a man that is a fornicator all bread is sweet,
> > he will not be weary of sinning unto the end.
> Every man that passeth beyond his own bed,
> > despising his own soul, and saying: Who seeth me?...
> And he knoweth not that the eyes of the Lord
> > are far brighter than the sun,
> beholding round about all the ways of men,
> > and the bottom of the deep,
> and looking into the hearts of men,
> > into the most hidden parts. (Sir 23:24-25, 28)[5]

You have been bought and paid for. Jesus is caring and loving. He always takes care of those whose ransom he paid. His sacrifice, his crucifixion, His death and resurrection, defines their full value. That's why he purchased them, to care for them, and perfect them within His kingdom in a corrupted

---

[5] In the Latin Vulgate and the Douay-Rheims, these verses are numbered as verses 24-25 and 28 of Sirach (Ecclesiasticus) 23. In more recent translations, these verses are numbered as verses 23:17-18a, 19.

world, saturated by the sophistication and complexity of sexual sin.

Sensory delights within a uniquely profound sexual union is God's gift to Christian spouses. Its endless mystical pleasures—forever eluding the world—belong to us. Let us recognize and protect the sacredness of our gift that we may possess it fully, pleasing the Giver, and deepening our marital union with dimensions of the transporting and transforming wonder of ourselves being miraculously blended into one in spirit, and in flesh, and in God.

Friendship

Pagan philosophers, such as Cicero and Aristotle, speak of the special depth that friendship can open to us—that a friend is like a second self. Consider then the depth of friendship Christ opens to spouses with His words of life: "Have ye not read, that he who made man from the beginning, Made them male and female? And he said: For this cause shall a man leave father and mother, and shall cleave to his wife, and they two shall be in one flesh. Therefore now they are not two, but one flesh. What therefore God hath joined together, let no man put asunder" (Matt 19:4-6). Christ's mysterious and profound forging of a spiritual unity from two beings bonded in marriage goes beyond the ideal concept of "friend" identified by pagan philosophers. If Christian spouses, therefore, miss the dimension of friendship in their marriage, they are missing sanctified depths of delight and spiritual opportunity!

Much has been written about the attitudes and activities which nurture friendship in marriage, particularly the importance of taking time to be friends together. However, there is no guarantee to a Christian couple that simply spending time together will nurture their marital unity or deepen their spiritual understanding. Even the world attests to the impotence of this simple, superficial answer with the popular phrase "quality time." What Christian spouses need to understand is that their marital friendship is a unique relationship: its dimensions are profoundly expanded from two to three; there are not just two beings interacting but three—husband, wife, and Jesus. Therefore, there is the possibility of a profound spiritual nurturing of unity in even the common tasks and events of life if spouses share these moments in the consciousness of being two united souls living and moving and having their being within Christ. This consciousness can give value and joy to the common stuff of life like weeding the yard or talking over the morning headlines; imagine then the possibilities of watching a sunset together or reading and discussing a passage from a Christian work or the Bible. Husbands and wives in Christ need to cultivate this consciousness amidst the uncertain and erratic motions of daily life—becoming aware of themselves as beings spiritually engaged in the mystery of unity acting and speaking and breathing in God.

Cherish what God has united. The same way you stand in awe of the mystery of how God mystically unites us to Christ and to Himself in the Church through baptism, esteem this mystery of friendship which God creates between you and your spouse. We all have friends. We have old friends, make new friends, and meet friends of friends. Let your charity reach out to everyone, but your intimacy to only one—and the One who has joined you to that one.

There are many aims, motives, pretexts, and frivolous intentions which can tempt and mislead the weak in heart in matters of virtue and love. A spouse who allows him or her self to indulge in "harmless" social games with a member of the opposite sex all too easily becomes a pawn in someone else's game: the evil inclination in humanity can "stroke," feed, and manipulate blind and hungry hearts through flattery, subtle innuendos, and murmurings about dissatisfactions. Spiritually unperceptive or immature souls may be tempted to reach out inappropiately to burdened "friends" who seek guidance and support.

Therefore, be not deceived, but understanding: friends skirt on intimacy for they bare the thoughts of the heart. Beware of someone who courts your vanity with the deceptive bait of sensual praises or false merit-giving. These are tares dressed as wheat. Do not desire to be esteemed by anyone except your spouse. Be very careful when approached by someone of the opposite sex, other than your husband/wife, when the issues are of the heart.

There are lawful friendships, and there are worldly, fleshly friendships. Reaching out in charity is not bad, but it can be dangerous for the unperceptive and immature if it goes too far. Avoid being too intimate with others except in the fear of God and the truths which He expresses for our well being. Love your spouse and have a friend with whom you can share the fullness of life. Befriend your spouse and receive the most intimate of gifts: love, pure and sacred, imbued with profound and joyful dimensions by Him who has joined you together as husband, wife, and friends.

Long-Suffering

Patiently enduring spiritual conflict is a unique mark of the Christian. It is our redeemed nature, the nature of our Christian heritage, to bear sufferings and become stronger. "[T]his is the victory which overcometh the world, our faith" (1 John 5:4). There will be occasions in your marriage when conflicts—whether they are conflicts of opinion, values, priorities, or methods of living—will generate an air of emotional intensity in the marital atmosphere. Often, reason is not effective in resolving differences which are spiritual.

In examining our Lord's life, we see that His recourse was the privacy of prayer. This was His staying power. He endured because He loved, and love is the mightiest of forces. Problems may arise between you and your spouse, or problems can come from outside the marriage. They may be of a general nature between you and other family members. It may seem like a ceaseless grapple with no end in sight. Yielding to your lower passions—stubbornness, anger, pride, unreasonableness, indifference—will in no way usher in a solution or victory. As Christians, we have a unique and marvelous relationship with our Lord which allows us to bear sufferings quietly and patiently. Trials challenge our spiritual perseverance. But be encouraged: Christ bears with you against all conflicts which cause a person to weaken but, in another truth, are opportunities to gain strength in His Name. Your faith in Him is that vitally needed factor which binds you to His healing powers and strengthening love.

The life of St. Paul is an extraordinary example to us in longsuffering. Having done so much for the Lord throughout his ministry—the teachings to different churches, miracles performed, his arrest and beatings, being stoned, shipwrecked, viper bitten, receiving heavenly visions and revelations—he also got very ill. In his own words, he tells us in the second book of Corinthians that he was accused of weakness and ambition, to the point where he is driven to sound his own praises. Then he writes:

> And lest the greatness of the revelations should exalt me, there was given me a sting of my flesh, an angel of Satan, to buffet me. For which thing thrice I besought the Lord, that it might depart from me. And he said to me: My grace is sufficient for thee; for power is made perfect in infirmity. Gladly therefore will I glory in my infirmities, that the power of Christ may dwell in me. For which cause I please myself in my infirmities, in reproaches, in necessities, in persecutions, in

distresses, for Christ. For when I am weak, then am I powerful. (2 Cor 12:7-10)

St. Paul is truly our model for longsuffering!

Patiently, you and your spouse should always pray together to ascertain the true nature of your marriage and the marriage between Christ and His Bride, the Church. Patiently pray for one another and accept the purification of your faith with long-suffering as a God-sent, allowed lesson which instructs, strengthens, encourages, and delivers us into eternal values. Married couples must continue to humbly communicate and persevere in loving patience while waiting for unstable emotional weather to pass. Quietly suffering is not an end in itself. It is a pathway for healing.

Encouragement in Trials and Temptations

Children, be forewarned: do not avoid dealing with your trials. Even though you have seen me studying the lives of many, many saints to understand their victories and you've listened to me speak so often about them, not one of them was entirely free and secure from temptations and trials while alive on earth. Trials and temptations are in store for all of us. Before I married your mother, I left my life of living in the city and went to live in the wilderness. I lived alone in dense tropical forests and in caves on ridges in isolated areas of Kauai's remote shores. I did this so I could leave behind me all the temptations and trials of the flesh and the world congested with the weaknesses of sins of fallen humanity. But to my dismay, I discovered even while alone, all by myself, I was my greatest enemy. I discovered I had a weak will which favored self instead of God. Although I had nothing external to distract or tempt me, I robbed myself of victory. There was a desire within me to live a good life, but the enemy was also within me and at times overpowered me. Thus, the struggle of laying down my will and living God's will taught me what dying unto self and living God's will really meant.

The struggle for spiritual mastery comes when the flesh,

of itself, is determined to remain rooted in its habits, refusing to yield to the truths and behavior of virtuous thought and conduct. The evil ways of the flesh and the world are the obstacles preventing God's grace from reshaping us anew into His likeness and image. Do you want to overcome the ways of the world? You must begin by learning to live a humble life of love.

Trials and temptations are not necessarily evil experiences. God in His infinite wisdom allows trials and temptations to those He loves so that their faith may be strengthened and purified. Abraham, Job, and our Savior Jesus Christ, are the ultimate examples of this test. History records many others. The lesson as the Apostle John teaches it is: "[T]his is the victory which overcometh the world, our faith" (1 John 5:4). By practicing a life of faith, a person directs his or her life to that avenue where God awaits His children with gifts of grace and redemption. Abandon your faith and you abandon the avenue of help which could have strengthened and delivered you victoriously in your severest hour of trial. Our Lord carefully explains this when discussing the parable of the sower to His disciples:

> Now the parable is this: The seed is the word of God. And they by the way side are they that hear; then the devil cometh, and taketh the word out of their heart, lest believing they should be

saved. Now they upon the rock, are they who when they hear, receive the word with joy: and these have no roots; for they believe for a while, and in time of temptation, they fall away. (Luke 8:11-13)

"They fall away," He says. And why? Shallow roots! In their desperation for relief, as well as their refusal to bear their yoke, they abandon the trial or succumb to temptation.

Christian spouses, do you want your marriage to last? Then remember the mystical gift of marital oneness is susceptible to a host of temptations and trials. God's intent is for a husband and wife to grow and mature in love and unity, but Satan's goal is to divide the spouses and destroy the relationship. Therefore, establish your "roots" in—and before—the time of trial. Turn your heart to the Lord when tempted, and guide yourself away from the calls of darkness by listening to His truths in the innermost depths of your being. Be patient with your spouse when he or she encounters the hour of temptation and trial. As Christ remains gentle and patient with you during your hour or day of trial, be of the same mind towards others.

Our Lord said to the Samaritan woman, "But the water that I will give him, shall become in him a fountain of water, springing up into life everlasting" (John 4:14). By His word, we have within each one of us that "fountain springing up into life everlasting." This confidence can strengthen us: temptations in themselves are no sin if we do not yield to their calling. Remember—when being tempted for whatever reason and especially by a member of the opposite sex—that within you is a spiritual well of moral goods which can help you overcome a desire to yield. Don't be overconfident or presumptuous; this will cause you to deceive yourself about your own powers. Temptations prove your true worth. Fear God when approaching that "inner fountain" from whence you need to draw your resources. Be genuinely humble; the devil cannot conquer genuine humility, for he himself cannot be humble.

No person, according to sacred scripture, is allowed to be tempted beyond his or her ability to endure. "And God is faithful, who will not suffer you to be tempted above that which you are able: but will make also with temptation issue, that you may be able to bear it" (1 Cor 10:13). Thus, know that, if you will it, you can endure by establishing your roots in the fertile promises of His word: you shall be victorious, and your joy shall be everlasting.

Finances

Money, the lack or excess of it, coupled with loose or thoughtless spending habits, is said to be one of the principal causes of separation and divorce. In the Jewish marriage ceremony, it has been customary since ancient times to read a Ketuba (wedding contract) during the wedding ceremony, obligating the husband to support his wife. Most variations can be summed up with these words: *I shall work for you, honor you, support and maintain you, in accordance with the custom and traditions of Jewish husbands who, in truth, work for their wives and honor them and support and maintain them.*

In today's world, earning a living is not the sole province of the husband; being a wife and mother is no longer an obstacle to gaining an income. Therefore, the intent of the Ketuba now applies equally to the husband and wife, though the nature of the "support and maintenance" and the balance of duties will be unique to each couple. Each will create their own division of labor in harmony with the unique combination of gifts and talents, workplace demands and pressures, idiosyncrasies and dislikes they bring to their union. The husband may cook, and wife may tune up the family vehicles; both may work outside the home or neither. But each will—equally—work for their spouse, honoring and supporting him or her.

The ideal home can be shattered by a multitude of economic considerations resulting from a consumer-oriented society, materialistic values, inordinate spending appetites, reduced finances, and other causes. It is imperative that both husband and wife agree on how the finances are to be handled. Financial priorities should be mutually agreed upon, then consistently reevaluated and maintained. In a society which preaches and chases money, wise asset management is essential in keeping harmony and understanding between a husband and wife. A severe lack of money due to the irresponsibility and/or negligence of either spouse, especially if compounded by global, national, or local financial strain, can harm the spirit and weaken the bonds of a marital unity. There is no doubt about the spirituality of a marriage in which a Christian husband and wife delight in their fervent love for each other; at the same time, however, they must exercise an adequate, consistent pragmatism and practicality in support of spouse, family, and related financial responsibilities. Most importantly, both must give money its proper value: it is only a tool, an implement, by which priorities and practical obligations are met.

As Christians, Christ wills us to be in the world, but not of it. Likewise, our marriage is to be in the world, but not of it. Proper financial management with mutual commitment is necessary if we are to successfully "be in the world": *success* meaning that we pragmatically protect and support a mystical spiritual union the world can never know; *success* meaning we are able to remain in the world that we may fulfill and possess the most profound possibilities—beyond the world's power to give—which He has envisioned and wills for our marriage.

Pleasure

Too much pleasure is like too much wine. Both can ruin the health of the body and injure and perhaps destroy the soul. Hedonism and debauchery corrupt the soul and rot the purity of the spirit. The defilement of any of the soul's faculties will inevitably cause an imbalance to the complementary functions. Overindulgence in food, alcohol, sex—habitual overgratification of the senses in any form—not only injures the body but also weakens the will, confuses the intellect, and distorts the appetites and desires. Immoderate sensory pleasures rob the soul of imagination and memory, working against and potentially rendering impotent Heaven's intention to offer the finer and nobler gifts from God.

It is true that the world around us is a gift and through our senses we perceive the realities which exist. It is also true that there is a world which we cannot see or sense but in which we must believe. That is the hidden world of tomorrow, Paradise and Heaven. Moderation permits us to thank God in a healthy way for the lawful pleasures bestowed upon us: eating, drinking, being merry, and sexually enjoying our spouses. Imbalanced desires for the entertainments of the sensory world will not only rob us of happiness in the world to come but can also have calamitous results in the uncertainties of the here and now.

Life is not all sensual, nor is it all physically perceived. Life is virtue. It is hope. It is faith. It is prayer. It is humility. It is mercy. It is study and discipline. But, most of all, life is love. Do not spend your energies nor waste time seeking and chasing excessive pleasures of the mind and body.

Christian spouses should be sensitive to each other's likes and dislikes, investing their time and energy in those activities which afford mutual enjoyment. Love each other, and together enjoy those lawful pleasures approved by God as genuine sources of happiness and virtue. To remain united in the joys of your marriage is a great joy unto Him. Pray together often: your raptures and delights will be peaceful. Be moderate in all pleasures so your souls can balance the conduct of your bodies.

Remember, as Christians you hold two citizenships: one of this world which your senses perceive and one of the world to come which you cannot see but in which you must believe. As you mature with age and grow in the Spirit, you will discover that there is lasting pleasure awaiting you in the mysteries of the faith. These are spiritual delights which can never be discovered by the external senses and the body. They can only be known by obedience to His word, with a sincere and humble heart. And with these, there can be no over-indulgence:

they give only life.

Lukewarm Love

The Biblical thought which comes to mind when considering the problem of "lukewarm love" is recorded in the Book of Revelation when the Risen Christ directs the Apostle John to write to the Seven Churches in Asia. John's admonition to the Laodicean Church:

> These things saith the Amen, the faithful and true witness, who is the beginning of the creation of God: I know thy works, that thou art neither cold, nor hot. I would thou wert cold, or hot. But because thou art lukewarm, and neither cold, not hot, I will begin to vomit thee out of my mouth. Because thou sayest: I am rich, and made wealthy, and have need of nothing: and knowest not, that thou art wretched, and miserable, and poor, and blind, and naked. (Rev 3:14-17)

Christ intends a dedicated, fervent, interactive love between Himself and His Church. The lukewarm Laodiceans, and others like them, He spits out of His mouth. In the same way, God intends marriage to be a sublime and spiritually dynamic experience continuously reimbued with fresh graces of the Almighty's love—which is never lukewarm.

There is much excitement and curiosity when lovers first marry. Love is desirable, thrilling, provocative, and alluring. Yet the long-term commitment—sickness and health, good times and bad—implies the possibility of gradual cooling into indifference. Often in the rush and push of daily practical concerns, our vision, values, and priorities upend and we are unaware of our slow impoverishment: "You say to yourself, 'I am rich, I have made a fortune, and have everything I want', never realizing that you are wretchedly and pitiably poor..." When indifference becomes the daily spiritual temperature of our marital relationship and our spouses are no longer desirable, problems are beginning to take root spiritually.

What can we do to prevent this slide into a dangerous lukewarmness? Study Christ in His relationship with His Bride: Christ talks to His Church hourly, daily, about His marriage to Her. He speaks through sacred scriptures, liturgies, rituals, prayerbooks, songs, and meaningful services. Correspondingly, spouses regenerate their relationship through communication. By discussing conflicts and disappointments, barren areas in a marriage are renourished and enriched: problems are weeded out before they take root and cause love to grow lukewarm and sickly.

Listen attentively to each other. Acknowledge the mutual respect due to each other. Purify your love with virtue to protect it from becoming lukewarm. Pray for one another. Love one another as Christ loves each of us. His love for all is so fervent that He died for the whole of humanity that each may experience the intensity and fullness of God's rich love.

It has never been recorded in sacred scripture that God, through His prophets or Christ, performed an act of lukewarm love for His people. Be Christ-minded when loving your spouse. Be thankful that love is God's gift to us, and we are His gifts to each other. Love each other with the same fervent purity that God uses when loving all that He has made.

Competitiveness

Sometimes, subtly, an air of competition develops between husband and wife. This is a dangerous atmosphere conducive to the undermining of marital unity. A husband and wife must not strive against each other. Rivalry can only give birth to dark and bitter emotions. According to Shakespeare, you don't want to open yourself to thoughts of jealousy: it will create a dark and bitter monster within you. Nothing good can come of attempting to be superior over one's spouse.

Competitive thoughts are motivated by what Jewish theology terms the "Yetzer-Hara"—the Evil Inclination. Such thoughts spring from a wrong or deluded attitude: allowing the world's definition and structuring of success to seep in and impose itself upon the sacred spiritual union of two souls. The world defines success as "me over you." One's success quotient is directly related to how many people one is "better than." We often hear of "the ladder of success": the world structures reality as a hierarchy—we trample over each other on the way to the top.

Marriage, however, is not a hierarchy but a unity. Spouses don't win over each other, but over temptation, sin, and illusion. If they're competing against each other, they're in the wrong battle and the wrong war. Husband and wife are allies: the gifts, talents, and blessings of each are properties and goods held in common. One's strength is the other's strength; one's glory is the other's. It is necessary for spouses to put on the mind of Christ, as St. Paul says in 1 Corinthians 2:16, sharing His mind, His way of thinking, and understanding themselves no longer as parts but as a spiritual whole.

Competitive thoughts undermine the profound mystery of God's spiritual knitting of two souls into one. In His unfathomable wisdom and power, He causes the strength of one spouse to supply the weakness of the other, and vice-versa. We need to be of understanding minds, therefore, and cooperate with God in the working out of this mystery. Rejecting competitive thoughts, we must become each other's gardener, concerned with nurturing and cultivating our spouse's talents, strengths, and blessings into perfect fruition.

Meanness

Meanness is, unfortunately, not uncommon in marriage: a word or action is directed from one spouse toward another with the sole intent of disturbing or wounding. Unkindness can take on many appearances, lurking behind a variety of deceptive human acts. Spouses often disguise their spiritual rancor under the pretext of a friendly or witty verbal exchange. It is very easy to appear polite to someone while your heart is filled with spite. One does not have to physically abuse another person to do injury. Caustic words can penetrate the soul, wounding the heart and clouding the spirit with vapors of pain. In many marriages—sadly—meanness is the "order of the day," the underlying impetus for most of the daily interaction between husband and wife.

What do we, as spouses, lose when we allow the substance of our communication to be dictated by spite? When we give ourselves up to meanness, all we are left with is our own bitterness. Joy flees; peace flees; intellectual/spiritual communion flees; gaiety, mirth, discovery, and wonder all flee: we bankrupt our marriage. Are we so deluded that we believe this is actually what we want? If in a moment of spiritual clarity, amidst the pullings and tearings of hurt and spite, we perceive this to be a poor bargain, then we need power to replace the habits of meanness with the behaviors of love: kindness, patience, and gentleness.

Go therefore to the Source: place yourselves before your Maker who has the wisdom and unfathomable power to reach into your hearts and change things. He can give you power—in that critical moment when some hurt is pulling and tearing at your insides, sorely tempting you to lash out like a wounded animal—to refuse to serve the clamoring voices of "righteous" bitterness.

Together, spouses need to consciously identify meanness as an extremely dangerous adversary capable of stealing away the profoundest and richest dimensions of their love. Fencing their hearts with charity and prayer, remaining spiritually wide awake and turning quickly from any temptations toward spite, husband and wife can protect the wonder, delight, and intellectual/spiritual communication of their God-given love.

Doubt

With all the pragmatic pressures of day-to-day living and the subtle temptations and undercurrents of spiritual warfare, it is easy for husband and wife to become divided amidst shifting vapors of doubt. Spouses may doubt each other—one another's intentions, perspectives, or choices; they may doubt their marital life—its directions, circumstances, or worth. These two aspects of doubt are inextricably bound up with a third: a doubtful faith. The three feed on and feed each other.

Therefore, as spouses, you must be spiritually militant–quick to recognize and deal effectively with manifestations of doubt. The first part of your offensive must be prayer. Should you begin to doubt each other's intentions, values, and love, remove that uncertainty by invoking together the Name of our God. Call upon Him in each other's presence, praying to reestablish the belief of your love and marriage. Pray for a clearing of vision, a harmonizing of one another's needs, desires, and goals. Place before God the weight of decisions made and those yet to be made. If it is not possible to pray together, then pray alone.

Second, talk and listen. Speak to each other honestly about those areas where doubts are pooling, breeding mistrust and fear. The dark vapors lose their power and dissipate when exposed to the rays of honest communication between kindred souls.

Third, be patient when solutions, clarity of vision, or complete harmony is not immediately forthcoming. Remember that each of you possesses only one-third of the answer, sees only one-third of the vision: one-third belongs to your spouse and one-third belongs to your Lord. That's the way He set things up—the reason why there are two parts to the marital whole and why humans possess a recalcitrant but spiritually educable free will. Therefore, be content at times to exist in a state of faithful uncertainty—praying and interacting and waiting on the Lord. You will know the difference between this state and that of doubt: the latter drags you down into confusion and, eventually, a dangerous isolation from each other and from the Lord—more dangerous still because it may seem that you are drawing closer to God by drawing apart from your spouse; the former buoys up your faith in each other and the Lord, deepening and enriching your love.

Evil Thoughts

Always remember that no good thing comes from evil thoughts or actions. Evil is wickedness and shamefulness—something detestable, foul, and abusive: evil harms. Evil manifests itself in more than action; it can be a feeling, thought, or idea. It can permeate fleeting emotional and mental impressions which then compound into an "opinion." In marriage there will be times when such opinions—evil thoughts about each other—create a potion of spiritual sickness, disrupting the peace and unity of love.

You are married because it is God's power which bonds your love for each other into a single body of both practical and mystical experiences. St. Paul writes of the virtues and actions in which God-given love manifests itself:

> Charity is patient, is kind: charity envieth not, dealeth not perversely; is not puffed up; Is not ambitious, seeketh not her own, is not provoked to anger, thinketh no evil; Rejoiceth not in iniquity, but rejoiceth with the truth; Beareth all things, believeth all things, hopeth all things, endureth all things. (1 Cor 13:4-7)

Resist evil thoughts with the manifestations of love St. Paul identifies and the Spirit empowers us to wield. Be spiritually alert: dark insinuations require silent, hidden, interior places to breed into power. Therefore, daily—continuously—allow the light of God's truth to penetrate the recesses of your heart in prayer. Ask the Holy Spirit to help you examine evil persuasions with the holy mind of Christ. Do not neglect to pray and talk with your spouse. If an issue is emotionally charged, be wise in choosing your time, and preface your discussion with prayer.

Sometimes we are not the authors of the evil thoughts which assail our minds. Be spiritually astute: recognize these times, and entrust your heart and intellect to what you know to be just and true.

Empty your hearts of any evil thoughts which you may harbor. Remember, marriage is a complex miracle developed by stages. Hope for the best, be patient with each other, and pray for love. Bitter, suspicious thoughts are mutually destructive: spiritually toxic to both your souls and to your love. Understand the human drama according to God's ways: evil thoughts can have no place in a relationship of sanctified marital love. For love takes no pleasure in the sins, weaknesses, or faults of another but, rather, hopes and works for corrections leading to reconciliation in the Peace of Christ. This is how Jesus loves each of us and how, as Christian spouses, we must love each other.

Rejection

Sometimes the choices spouses make creates conflicts in their relationship: decisions made by a husband may hurt his wife or a wife's preferences may offend her husband; the actions of one may offend the values of the other. Careless choices may lead to misunderstanding and anger. Without a bridge of prayer and communication, this emotional/spiritual/intellectual rift may widen into rejection of one spouse by the other. Given the long-term and intimate commitment of marriage, a spouse is likely to experience, at least briefly, both roles: the one who rejects and the one who is rejected. Spouses need a spiritual understanding of the temptations and powers at work in both sides of rejection so that they can turn this marital pitfall into a strengthening and deepening of their love.

When you find yourself tempted to reject your spouse, it is vital and empowering to focus on the sacrifice of Christ—He whose desire was to die in His love that we would be set free to love the Father with Him. Imagine how it must pain the Sacred Heart of Jesus when we, the Church, reject His love, His sacrifice for us. Similarly, be mindful that there is no greater pain in holy matrimony than the rejection of one spouse's love by the other. When wrestling with the hurt inflicted through your spouse's ignorance, weakness, and/or selfishness, remember that God has not given up on that person and therefore you must not either.

Rejection is far too absolute to be safely wielded by anyone except the God of perfect justice. It implies, first of all, rejection not of an action or behavior but of a person—a human soul who is still a developing part of God's plan. Therefore, reject ignorant, weak, or selfish behaviors but never one another. Second, there is a finality to rejection: it implies no more possibilities—no more windows to be opened for that soul by His grace. But God does not give up on souls; He is still working with your spouse and will give you the grace to do so too. We must actively bear with one another, in the same way as Christ bears with us.

Conversely, when you find yourself caught in the opposite role—suffering the pain of being rejected—remember to pray with interior examination. Ask God for spiritual self-insight; do what you can to identify and reverse those behaviors which may be causing pain and confusion for your spouse. Ask also for patience that you avoid the temptation of returning rejection for rejection but, instead, abide in a good spirit until God works within your spouse to the point where communication is again possible.

Beyond this, be of this mind:

> Blessed be the God and Father of our Lord Jesus Christ, the Father of mercies, and the God of all comfort. Who comforteth us in all our tribulation; that we also may be able to comfort them who are in all distress, by the exhortation wherewith we also are exhorted by God. (2 Cor 1:3-4)

Our human nature reacts to the disappointment and uncertainty of a dark situation—to feelings of isolation and helplessness—with cries of self-pity. But as those who have died and risen with Christ, we are no longer enslaved by our fallen natures. Therefore, resist self-pity: turn your mind and energies to the sufferings which others must bear—including your spouse. Pray for their consolation and deliverance with the same earnestness you pray for your own. As St. Francis of Assisi prayed, "grant that I may not so much seek to be consoled as to console." Be patient and gentle with all who suffer even though their pain is a result of their own neglect, ignorance, weakness, or sin. If you do not reject the sufferings of others, He who is our Consoler will not judge and reject you in the time of your need.

Husbands and wives who find themselves caught in the trap of rejecting each other need to consciously and spiritually deal with the powers and temptations that are at work on them. With God's help, they can turn rejection around, using it to strengthen and enrich their unity.

The Pain of Disappointment

Because Christian marriage is an intimate and long-term relationship, husbands and wives will inevitably come to those moments when they are disappointed in themselves and, at other times, in their spouses. Both aspects of disappointment are painful. It is not an easy experience to face and admit our guilt to ourselves without qualification and then seek forgiveness of another human being for the hurt we have caused them. Neither is it easy to put on the mind of Christ: bearing with your spouse as she/he disappoints you; resisting bitter, vengeful thoughts; putting your spouse's spiritual welfare ahead of your own hurt and attempting to hold nothing back in your heart when you say "I forgive you."

Pain of the body and pain of the spirit are different sorts: a scar of the body after it is healed no longer hurts; in contrast, a scar of the spirit, when brought forth by the memory, recalls some of the spiritual pain which caused it. Therefore, in marriage, disappointment and its bruises must be faced and worked through before guilt, bitterness, and/or resentment fester and scar. Disappointment can be overcome if we take on the struggle within our Lord: "Come to me, all you that labour, and are burdened, and I will refresh you. Take up my yoke upon you, and learn of me, because I am meek, and humble of heart: and you shall find rest to your souls" (Matt 11:28-29). As we seek grace from the bountiful providence of God, we can prevail over our frustrations and bitterness.

When we are disappointed in ourselves and laden with guilt, then prayer, penance, reparation, and practicing the presence of Christ in our daily lives with the aid of His sacraments are the most useful actions we can perform to achieve peace with clean hearts. When afflicted with pain from any sort of disappointment—in ourselves or each other—think of the Suffering Servant, Jesus, who suffered while innocent of any crime attributed to Him. Recall too that there is always another human being whose grief and tribulation exceed your own. Focus on tragedies greater than yours; pray for others whose marital problems are in need of healing. Your spirits will be refreshed, your pains lessened, and your confidence in God's timely solutions steadied. The peace of Christ which passes all understanding will cover your disappointments and bring you a renewed and joyful outlook.

Anger

The wise King Solomon admonishes us with this lesson: "Hatred stirreth up strifes: and charity covereth all sins" (Pr. 10.12). Unchecked anger engenders a venomous license of the tongue, bringing turmoil and injury to the spirit. A thoughtless and harshly spoken word is like a spark igniting a small flame which in turn sets the whole forest ablaze: an untimely word, bitterly spoken, maliciously intended, wounds the heart and fills the injured mind with venomous and painful thoughts. If left unchecked, misunderstandings compound misunderstandings, creating hostility and insecurity in a marriage.

Again King Solomon cautions us to be careful with our speech: "Death and life are in the power of the tongue: they that love it, shall eat the fruits thereof" (Prov 18:21). The spiritual fact is that our tongues have the power to bring forth the fruits of life or death—and if we could rule our tongues so that our words are life-giving, we must keep our hearts with all diligence and away from anger. St. Paul, in admonishing the Ephesians, states:

"Let all bitterness, and anger, and indignation,

> and clamour, and blasphemy, be put away from you, with all malice. And be ye kind one to another; merciful, forgiving one another, even as God hath forgiven you in Christ." (Eph 4:31-32)

Through the Holy Spirit, God gives us the grace to obey His Words of Life if we turn to Him with humble and sincere hearts. When you are the cause of anger, be humble and prepared to seek forgiveness. Think to yourself: "Lord, if I am the cause of evoking anger and bitterness from another, grant me the grace to seek forgiveness for the injury I have caused." And if it is against you that anger is vented by another in his or her moment of unrighteousness, pray that the Lord make you an instrument of His peace. If your spouse permits dark options—wanderings of the imagination with negative impulses and excesses of bitterness, anger and revenge—to cloud your love for each other, try to think of Jesus' words in the Sermon on the Mount:

> But I say to you, Love your enemies: do good to them that hate you: and pray for them that persecute and calumniate you: That you may be the children of your Father who is in heaven, who maketh his sun to rise upon the good, and bad, and raineth upon the just and the unjust. (Matt 5:44-45)

It is a person's opportunity to become spiritually mature when confronted by negative impulses coming from someone venting an unjust anger.

The power of the Spirit is always upon us; but at times, when the trials of life seem to inundate us, we can be totally obtuse to that fact. Thus, in our marriages, when our problems seem overwhelming and solutions appear to be beyond the horizon of understanding, we must seize His grace. We must become persons of faith and prayer, seeking transformation of our anger into love.

Sirach (132 BC) clarifies the spiritual laws we set in motion through our choice of either anger or understanding:

Anger and fury are both of them abominable,
    and the sinful man shall be subject to them.
He that seeketh to revenge himself,
    shall find vengeance from the Lord,
    and he will surely keep his sins in remembrance.
Forgive thy neighbour if he hath hurt thee:
    and then shall thy sins be forgiven to thee when thou prayest.

Man to man reserveth anger,
    and doth he seek remedy of God?
He hath no mercy on a man like himself,
    and doth he entreat for his own sins?
He that is but flesh, nourisheth anger,
    and doth he ask forgiveness of God?

who shall obtain pardon for his sins? (Sir 27:33-28:5) [6]

Keeping Sirach's advice in mind, we must remember to turn from anger to our proper senses by recalling ourselves to spiritual sobriety. Such actions are within our power with the help of His grace. Therefore, before venting your anger and flooding your spouse's spirit with bitterness, prayerfully seek a peaceful way to express yourself even though your opinions may be opposed by your spouse's attitude. Although this way may not be characteristic and comfortable to your sinful and fallen nature, it need not bring vexation to your spirit. Express yourself with composure, and your spouse's unwarranted anger will see its own folly in the mirror of its angry spirit.

---

[6] In the Latin Vulgate and the Douay-Rheims, these verses are numbered as 27:33-28:5 of Sirach (Ecclesiasticus). In more recent translations, these verses are numbered as verses 27:30-28:5.

Vanity

> Nothing under the sun is new, neither is any man able to say: Behold this is new: for it hath already gone before in the ages that were before us. There is no remembrance of former things: nor indeed of those things which hereafter are to come, shall there be any remembrance with them that shall be in the latter end. (Eccl 1:10-11)

God deals in paradox. From this passage in Ecclesiastes, God wants us to realize that nothing is new and that all things pass away. This is the key to understanding and rendering impotent the powerful spiritual force of vanity. Those who have allowed themselves to become slaves to vanity have given a false importance to their personal qualities, talents, and ambitions. To God, our Maker who died for us, each person is of infinite importance—but within the context of the vast, monumental spiritual realities of which that person is a part. Those who subject themselves to their own vanities are attempting to create and constantly re-prove their importance and glory outside of God's plan and the spiritual movement and structure that the Creator and human free will have set in motion.

When the Prophet Jeremiah rebuked the Israelites for their apostasy, this is one of the statements he declared: "Thus saith the Lord: What iniquity have your fathers found in me, that they are gone far from me, and have walked after vanity, and are become vain?" (Jer 2:5).

The vain person refuses to acknowledge the realities he/she can see being proven and reproven all around him/her: the inescapable fact that everything grows old—a irreversible process ended by death; the fact that each animal has a specific talent or gift, but none has every or even most talents and gifts—each can do a small thing miraculously well; the fact that self-created ambitions and moments of glory are mirages of satisfaction constantly replacing themselves. The weight of one's life passes like mist. The vain person doggedly insists on spinning his wheels in illusion, saying "Look now, my glory is new," and "Behold, my glory shall not pass." In this way, vanity is hypocrisy's twin. Those who insist on subjecting themselves to their own vain illusions will become vagabond characters with unsettled spiritual natures and lives irresponsibly adrift.

God has given the human free will the power to live and die ineffectually in self-created illusions—to pass without ever connecting with God's plan or with the movement and structure of spiritual reality. But when we refuse to understand our personal qualities, talents, and importance from God's perspective and instead busy ourselves preening and protecting and proving the validity of self-created glory, we miss the genuine glory God has placed in us and wants to accomplish through us. The extent to which we actively self-create glory is the extent to which we willfully forfeit the real thing.

This can have disastrous results in a marriage. The spiritual union effected by God between two souls is a part and type of His plan—set down before the foundations of the earth were laid—towards a perfect Oneness of all created and non-created things within His Truth and Love. If marriage, by its spiritual nature, draws its substance and reality from this Plan, yet husband and wife are busily engaged in pursuing vain activities outside this Plan, conflict is inevitable. The spouse who pours unnecessary amounts of mental energy, time, and money into an image presented to the world; the husband/wife who has to exercise beyond genuine health requirements at the expense of family time; the spouse who is so wrapped up in personal ambitions that there is no time or energy for marital ambitions—intellectual/spiritual/physical sharing and vision; the husband/wife who plays "harmless" games of flirtation, betraying a spouse's love for a brief, self-glorifying "stroke" by a stranger. As spouses become more and more engrossed in self, they become less and less able to enjoy or appreciate or share with or even "see" each other—and frequently, it's the marriage which is abandoned.

Therefore, rather than hungering for the compliments of the flesh and the world—arousing vanity in your spirit—

glory instead in the Lord. Are we not taught to pray that "Thine is the kingdom, the power, and the glory for ever and ever"? This being the truth, let His power be your glory so that your developing soul may rest in His kingdom and invest itself in His plan rather than chasing the empty, transitory glories of the world, wasting its days in self-delusion. We need to stop focusing on ourselves—our ambitions and brief, personal glories—and begin consistently refocusing on the Lord. As we recur to Him—to His perspectives of truth and love and His eternal plan—we discover the real glory He has given us and the mystical glory hidden in the love we share with our spouse.

Married Image and Appearance

As a high-tech society, America runs on "image." T.V., magazines, music videos persuade us to see image and appearance as reality; sophisticated advertisements barrage us with the critical importance of checking, creating, and improving our own image. Psychologists have identified the step from innocence into experience as that point when a child first becomes aware of how the world is looking at him/her: that moment when he realizes that he is an identity separate from mother/father/environment and steps outside to look at himself as someone else—the world—perceives him (or her). America is steeped in—promotes and pushes—this step into "experience": our children take that step early.

When Adam and Eve fell from innocence, they immediately saw themselves and covered up—it was out of their need to hide their guilt from their God. As Christians, we are followers of the new "Adam." Dying with Him, we are spiritually reborn into the likeness of Christ: we receive a new image, one He commands us to—daily more and more—"put on." He admonishes us to to be aware of our spiritual "image": to check, evaluate, and perfect our likeness of Christ.

> For if a man be a hearer of the word, and not a doer, he shall be compared to a man beholding his own countenance in a glass. For he beheld himself, and went his way, and presently forgot what manner of man he was. But he that hath looked into the perfect law of liberty, and hath continued therein, not becoming a forgetful hearer, but a doer of the work; this man shall be blessed in his deed. (Jas 1:23-25)

As Christian spouses, our bodies animate the personality and character of the heaven-sent spirituality which indwells and moves us; therefore, we should be humbly concerned with our representation of self in Christ—the representation of being a faithful, modest husband or wife in Him. Christ-like love is humble and redemptive. Love originating purely from self is proud, haughty, and spiritually self-destructive. Vain love contributes to hypocrisy—to the wearing of a mask. As a husband or wife in Christ, you must avoid the worldly illusions of mask-wearing, of putting on a self-made image fueled by a self-glorifying ego. The consequences can be costly when reality is somehow unavoidable, and the mask is exposed.

Life-giving, spiritually healthy love becomes visible as selfish love fades and disappears, dying in sacrifice for the lover. The mystical richness of this sacrifice nurtures and purifies a husband's and wife's love for each other. Thus, sanctified marital love slowly images the love which Christ has for His Bride, the Church. This gradual manifestation changes the appearance of an ordinary marriage into the noble status of Holy Matrimony: the virtuous gifts of heaven's Spirit, such as patience, kindness, gentleness, and wisdom, take deepening root in the practical human love between husband and wife, providing them with spiritually fruitful lives here on earth.

The two significant traits of a married couple's image and appearance in Christ are singleness of heart and purity of heart. If there is this "single eye" in marriage—the vision of Holy Matrimony shared in good faith with mutual respect—then the single mystical and marital body of husband and wife will distill into a spiritual image of their love shining forth to others with the appearance of a sanctified unity.

Keep your love pure, your heart and eye single. Then will your marriage be sustained in holiness and joy, imaging the love Christ has for His Church. Learn to sacrifice for each other, and that image will surely form and shine.

Separation and Reconciliation

Reflecting on the issues of separation and reconciliation awakens thoughts of pain and joy. It also brings to mind the thoughts of St. Paul:

> For if, when we were enemies, we were reconciled to God by the death of his Son; much more, being reconciled, shall we be saved by his life. And not only so; but also we glory in God, through our Lord Jesus Christ, by whom we have now received reconciliation. (Rom 5:10-11)

To separate means to divide or disunite—to tear apart. Imagine the grief the Jewish people suffered when, led into captivity, they were torn from their beloved Temple in Jerusalem where they had joyfully celebrated feast days and other happy occasions. The prophet Jeremiah indicts Judah and all the people of Jerusalem who, because of their failure to turn from evil, were to be separated from their land; Yahweh would use Nebuchadnezzar, King of Babylon, as his scourging tool (Jer 25:1-13). There are numerous Biblical illustrations showing us how Israel's sinful behavior ruptured and bruised the love between God and His chosen people. History's lesson is clear: sin separates, causing pain and darkness; reconciliation restores joy.

The divorce—tearing asunder—of Christian spouses is one of the deepest spiritual pains afflicting the Church. "What therefore God hath joined together" (Matt 19:6; Mark 10:9)—hearts, minds, wills, appetites and desires, emotions, and bodies—when torn apart, engenders a form of pain the complexity of which far exceeds rational definition. It can become a spiritually mystical nightmare. Avoid the agonies of separation: keep your love and marriage free from any sin that would affect your unity. For the pains of the body, medical science has developed painkillers. For the pains of the soul there is only one healing: mercy which comes with the precious Body and Blood of Jesus Christ.

Should separation occur for whatever reason, remember the sacred Body and Blood of Jesus Christ fills us "with joyful trust in God."

> But all things are of God, who hath reconciled us to himself by Christ; and hath given to us the ministry of reconciliation. For God indeed was in Christ, reconciling the world to himself, not imputing to them their sins; and he hath placed in us the word of reconciliation. For Christ therefore we are ambassadors, God as it were

exhorting by us. For Christ, we beseech you, be
reconciled to God. (2 Cor 5:18-20)

Appeal to God in fervent prayer as His injured child in need of the inflowing precious, healing life of Christ. Appeal as a former enemy, a willful sinner, who now as a penitent and obedient child to His will desires to receive Him and all that divinely belongs to Him: His mercy, love, healing, wisdom, and peace. Pray for restitution and restoration; seek good actions and do them with charity, for charity heals. Avoid sin and the dark persuasions of sin; pray that the presence of Christ will reconcile you to your spouse as you have been reconciled to God by the precious Body and Blood of Jesus Christ.

Through Jesus, the Sinless One, God offers Himself for the development of a new order—a new world. Therefore, pray for the restoration of an unblemished love. Pray for the joy of life and sacredness, the divinization of two becoming one.

Request the charity of Christ while being His ambassador of mercy and forgiveness to your spouse. Putting on this mind of Christ and being a minister of reconciliation requires the power and purity of His presence. As He has declared through His Apostle Paul, we should not hold faults against each other: we are to appeal in Christ's name that we might reflect the goodness of God. Together, settle your differences and quarrels intelligently as children whose Father is God:

replace the spirit of discontent by accommodating each other's needs with the joy of love and harmony. What has been forgiven should be forgotten.

Do not neglect the healing powers vested in the sacraments of reconciliation and the Holy Eucharist. Together, appear before Christ in prayer and devotion that He may restore to you the joy of life and your trust in the sacred, mystic reality of yourselves as husband and wife—the divinization of two becoming one.

Cultural Differences

Thine are the heavens, and thine is the earth:
the world and the fulness thereof thou hast founded... (Ps 88:12)[7]

It is possible that you may choose or have chosen to marry someone of another racial extraction with a cultural background different from your own. An alloy is strong: spouses in a bicultural marriage have the opportunity to see reality through each other's eyes, opening perspectives outside their own enculturated mindset and experience. It is fascinating, humbling, and broadening to discover afresh in new ways through the years that your way is not the only way, your understanding not the only viewpoint. A Christian husband and wife of different cultural backgrounds who successfully create unity out of their diversity have increased flexibility and resourcefulness for meeting the challenges of life, fascinating dimensions and depths to offer each other, and a tested empathy for one another's perspectives.

---

[7] In the Latin Vulgate and the Douay-Rheims, this verse is numbered as verse 12 of Psalm 88. In more recent translations, this verse is numbered as verse 11 of Psalm 89.

However, the flip-side of a bicultural marriage is that there is more diversity to harmonize into unity. What may seem trivial and unimportant to you may be precious and vital to your spouse. Cultural values and important customs and traditions which make up the social fabric of one society may not even exist within another. Ethnic differences go far deeper than foods or holiday traditions or family customs. All people are, to some degree, environmentally conditioned by the traditions and values of their society. From the moment we take our first breath, our cultural environment influences our personality—who we are—because it shapes the ways we perceive "reality" and ourselves in relation to "reality." Each individual's culture is part of the lens through which he/she views and makes sense of the world. That lens focuses and structures reality: how we "see" influences our values, priorities, and perspectives for it colors the ways we understand life and make meaning of our world. Spouses of divergent ethnic backgrounds, therefore, should be prepared for culturally spawned differences in concerns, fears, motivations, and ways of doing things.

As Christian spouses in a bicultural union become aware of a difference in values or perspective, they need to discuss the issue in an atmosphere of love and mutual respect. The social harmony of their marriage depends on their acknowledging and reconciling differing perceptions of day-to-day practical priorities and expectations. If they can recognize a disagreement as springing from cultural rather than spiritual disparity, they will be able to work through the conflict more effectively and less emotionally. Their educated faith and devout spiritual practices can provide a solid, shared foundation on which to build their marriage.

Catholic Christians visiting a foreign nation experience cultural diversities within the Holy Mass. Yet informed Catholics are not disturbed, but rather are free to enjoy these differences because they know the essential order of the Mass is universally approved by the Magisterium. Likewise, married couples can develop an agreed-upon marital magisterium, creating order, as the Church does, while incorporating and expressing the beauties—and truths—of the differences.

God is the source of humanity, and ethnic cultures are the exceptional gifts of humankind's traditions to each other. You and your spouse must seek out the culturally good in your backgrounds and, in Christ, share the bounty of your gifts to strengthen and colorfully imbue the bond of your love. Pray often together. Mutually present the depths of your hearts sincerely before the Lord with prayers for grace and forgiveness. Cultivate a deep-rooted trust while attempting to resolve any differences you may have. Patiently and politely observe and assess situations before objecting to something which appears disagreeable to your enculturated mindset, attitudes, and understanding. Be willing to laugh together to see the humor in your culturally created differences. Exercise a kindly disposition when attempting to understand any cultural incompatibility which may interfere with the peace and love of your marriage. Remember, it is the Lord God who joins husband and wife into "oneness." Therefore, you both must go to Him with all that you are, and He will refine the complexities of your developing unity.

Children

Children are the wonderful fruits of marriage. Like their parents, they are the inheritors of God's treasures, the repositories of His mysteries, nobly related to the hierarchies and dominions of His unfading Kingdom: God has no grandchildren, only children. A child is the window of tomorrow: he/she is the tomorrow of today's world. It is the faculties of our children's souls—their spiritually schooled free wills, hearts, and intellects—that will meet humanity's future needs by bringing to bear God's thoughts and actions on His continuing plan of love for the redemption of humankind.

Our children's identities and destinies lie in God. We are their stewards given to fence them about with care, love, and a spiritually grounded respect. Their souls are equal and identical to ours, both in the capacity for imaging the likeness—the glory—of God and in the vulnerability to "the evil impulse." Sin is not biologically inheritable but the *impulse* to sin is. Our children's souls are made up of the same spiritually fallen organic matter as ours; they, however, have the chance—the strength—we give them by educating them to the nature and consequences of sinful tempting persuasions. Their spiritual strengthening and maturation, laughter, and wonder are our sacred responsibility as parents. Family values of the heart—sharing, caring, patience, joy, spiritual knowledge, prayer, and worship—all play a part in our offspring's development as followers of Christ.

Providing knowledge and an education for our children are only partial provisions toward their intellectual development, for the intellect is a faculty of the soul. As heirs of Christ, our children should also be acquainted with—disciplined and exercised in—the ways of wisdom. A God-fearing heart and spiritually cultivated intellect along with a well-tended memory filled with the knowledge of God's people and history are gifts of life to any society, perpetuating its days with the substance of truth and vision.

As parents, we should be gentle and patient with instruction, yet firm, clear, and direct with correction. We must not be afraid of the things our offspring will see and hear and encounter as they become increasingly engaged with the world. Rather, we must recognize our sacred opportunity to stand with them during those fleeting childhood and adolescent years, lending them wisdom and perspective, vision and strength—giving them a spiritual stronghold to retreat into love when wounded—until they are wise and strong enough to go forth on their own and manifest in their lives Christ's profound command to be in the world but not of the world (John 15:18-19; 17:14-16).

By experiencing with our offspring a genuine life of faith, with its disciplines and conditioning, hope and joy, we are bequeathing them a tested spiritual vision: with God's grace, they too will see beyond the worldly folly of man's transient illusions and help to save others from spiritual deserts. Therefore, pray with your children and play with them as well. Listen as earnestly to their hearts' concerns as you expect them to listen to your instructions. Especially, love them throughout their trials and support them in time of failure. They are the flesh of your flesh and the posterity of your love. By God's grace, their hearts, which you fill today with parental love, will breathe prayers heavenward one day in your behalf. Laugh with them, wonder with them, and have fun together.

Reading

"What profit is there in reading and discussing together?" you and your spouse may ask, especially if you have precious little leisure time or are not used to thinking of yourselves as "readers" or "scholars." The benefits can be many—an experience repeatedly fresh with surprising blessings and rich with timely insights. By reading sacred scripture and other writings inspired in Christ, you can receive valuable lessons from the trials and sufferings of others. Those who have sacrificed their lives for the Lord and served His purposes reflect His presence in their lives. Their inspired words give spiritual instructions tested and proved in the flesh of the authors. As a husband and wife nurture and exercise their intellects and spirits with these holy authors, they can learn to retain these illumined gems of truth, using them to reflect on the darkened world about them.

Intellectual/spiritual intercourse is essential to the full development of the love affair between you and your spouse. No matter what educational background you bring to an inspired text, you always bring your heart, and God makes wise the simple. No matter what the challenges of the spiritual and textual landscape, you are well equipped enough to traverse together, discovering realities of worlds seen and not seen, opening and strengthening the truths in each other, and discerning the nature of your own spirits and identities in God. For we can never discover our identities in the world: no one out there can—or cares to—tell us who we are. Our identities lie hidden in God; only He can give them to us truly and lastingly. And marriage is one of the great doors of grace to finally answering the nagging question our Maker has embedded in our souls: "Who am I?"

Knowing demands effort. But more important, practicing what we learn makes us "one" with our knowledge. Marriage is a learning process. It offers us, as Christian spouses, continuous opportunities for intellectual and spiritual enrichment. To be fruitful, however, we must apply ourselves to virtuous practices stemming from our knowledge. Just as a farmer cannot harvest a quality crop from a field he has never tilled or planted, so we cannot possess the treasures revealed in our spiritual study and discussion without exercising ourselves in the disciplines suggested to us there.

Reading, contemplating, and discussing the inspired thoughts of faithful souls, you and your spouse can together develop the intellectual stronghold all Christian couples need to defend their beliefs in their sanctified spiritual union and in their love. During moments or extended seasons of need and conflict, you can draw from this repository, tapping into divine forces of grace through the written insights of the faithful. Always remember that all you learn of love will be supported by grace. This is your assurance that while you are sincerely learning of love, God is busily loving you.

In-Laws

Much of what is written on the "in-law problem" fails to address and draw insight from the dual nature of this issue: in marriage, generally, we not only acquire in-laws but also become them. A Biblical love story recorded in the Book of Tobit contains edification and gentle guidance which can help us conduct ourselves with Christian wisdom and charity as we walk in either or both of the "in-law" roles.

The story recounts the love of Tobias, son of Tobit and Anna, for Sarah, daughter of Raguel and Edna. When the two are married, the new father-in-law, Raguel, tells Tobias "...Take courage, son! I am your father, and Edna is your mother; we belong to you and to your sister both now and forever. So take courage, son!" (Tob 8:21 NAB). Again, when instructing Tobias and Sarah after the wedding feast as they prepare for their journey back to Tobit: "...Farewell, son. Have a safe journey. May the Lord of heaven grant prosperity to you and to your wife Sarah...." (Tob 10:11 NAB). To his daughter, Sarah, Raguel says, "...My daughter, honor your father-in-law and your mother-in-law, because from now on they are as much your parents as the ones who brought you into the world..." (Tob 10:12 NAB).

The lesson which Raguel conveys to Sarah is that she is now equally a daughter to Tobit and Anna as to her genetic parents. To Tobias, Raguel imparts the fact that he and Edna have become Tobias' parents. Christ's uniting of two souls in holy matrimony has bonded children and parents in an interactive network of mutual charity and respect.

Therefore, "be not conformed to this world; but be reformed in the newness of your mind" (Rom 12:2). As husband and wife, strive in prayer and action to accord your in-laws the dignity due their parental status. As in-laws (the perspective less often addressed), help Christ transform the biological bond between yourselves and your child into the spiritual bond between a man and a woman—a profound fruition—by adopting in prayer, thought, word, and action the following attitude:

> *Our child, flesh of our flesh, as your parents, we love and will support you in your marriage. However, we consider it our spiritual duty not to be partial to you because you are of our blood. You will become "one" with another human being. And as much as we may love you, financially provide for you, psychologically assist you, philosophically guide you, and theologically encourage you, we will not close our hearts or*

minds to the needs of your spouse.

When your marriage is tried by pressures and stressful circumstances and events, come to us but not alone: come with your spouse. Together present your difficulties. Avoid blaming your spouse before us if he/she is absent. The common tragedy of in-law partiality has no place in our hearts: it would be a sin for us to favor you, who may be at fault, without seeking to provide equal grace and comfort to your spouse.

Though we love you dearly, we must—by divine decree—love the whole "one" of you together. Indeed, our love for you is too great to allow us to assist "the evil influence" in widening the deceptive rift between you and that one to whom Christ has joined you. When your children marry, it will be the same with you to them, as with us to you, as with Raguel when he said to Sarah his daughter: honor your father-in-law and your mother-in-law, because from now on they are as much your parents as the ones who brought you into the world...[8]

As husband and wife, always pray for your in-laws; as in-

---

[8](Tob 10:12 NAB)

laws, always pray for your son and daughter: that, through them, God will visit you in your needs and, through you, He will care and provide for them. Pray that God will bless the whole family that all will bless each other with some happiness, love, wisdom, and charity.

Forgiveness

The act of forgiving is a spiritual issue which must have tried and is presently trying all people who, because of their spiritual limitations, understand so little of the full implication of mercy and forgiveness. The ultimate act and lesson of forgiveness and mercy has been revealed for all humanity—whether learned or simple—to understand:

> And when they were come to the place which is called Calvary, they crucified him there; and the robbers, one on the right hand, and the other on the left. And Jesus said: Father, forgive them, for they know not what they do. But they, dividing his garments, cast lots. (Luke 23:33-34)

Even after Jesus prayed for those who crucified Him, they persevered in their sinful ways by gambling for His clothes. Our Lord, in His prayer and freely accepted death, shows us what it means to forgive "seventy times seven."

In Christian marriage, inevitably, trivial and significant offences occur, and spouses hurt each other. Reconciliation and healing is often warped by the sin of pride. During the crucial and trying moments of their marriage, Christian spouses need to remember that, as children of the Most High, their spiritual conduct should mirror His image and likeness: "For thou, O Lord, art sweet and mild: and plenteous in mercy to all that call upon thee. Give ear, O Lord, to my prayer: and attend to the voice of my petition" (Ps 85:5-6).[9]

Like our Lord, you also must be good and forgiving. You also must listen attentively to your spouse's request for forgiveness, keeping in mind the spiritual principle Jesus teaches: "And forgive us our debts, as we also forgive our debtors" (Matt 6:12).

"But the line must be drawn," some will say—yet the spiritual law stands and will be exacted: "For with what judgment you judge, you shall be judged: and with what measure you mete, it shall be measured to you again" (Matt 7:2). We must remember that God's mercy for us extends far beyond the rational, reasonable, practical "judgment lines" which are the just due of our sinful actions. Therefore, we must not grow weary of compassion: "Bearing with one another, and forgiving one another, if any have a complaint against another: even as the Lord hath forgiven you, so do you also" (Col 3:13).

It is difficult to forgive someone when betrayal, violence, infidelity, and other grievous sins have caused severe wounds

---

[9] In the Latin Vulgate and the Douay-Rheims, these verses are numbered as verses 5-6 of Psalm 85. In more recent translations, these verses are numbered as verses 5-6 of Psalm 86.

in marriage. It is helpful to understand that forgiveness means you refuse to nurture bitter, vengeful thoughts in your heart; it does not necessarily mean you accept the situation—especially physical or emotional abuse. To forgive means to will to understand; it is an act of your unchanged commitment to becoming spiritually "one" with another human soul.

And when you sin—though your sins be not as serious as those mentioned above—how can you seek and rest in the Lord's forgiveness if within your heart mercy is distant, perhaps absent, and judgment lines are the rules and measures. Jesus gives us the spiritual truth that those who are unforgiving have not yet discovered God's mercy and forgiveness for themselves. Speaking to the Pharisee Simon about the "sinful" woman who has anointed His feet with ointment, Jesus says: "Wherefore I say to thee: Many sins are forgiven her, because she hath loved much. But to whom less is forgiven, he loveth less. And he said to her: Thy sins are forgiven thee" (Luke 7:47-48).

Evidently the lesson here also teaches us that those who know little of forgiveness know even less of love. The law of marriage is principally to love: to be "one." Spouses who lack mercy towards each other and know little of forgiveness will find their love shriveling, their unity dissolving. The virtues of mercy and forgiveness revive the spirit with a fresh breeze of love. Have you not felt refreshed in spirit when apologizing to someone for committing an offense against them? And when they accept your apology and desire to forget the event, does not their act of mercy lift your downtrodden spirit?

Forgiveness is more than forgetting because it is an act of the will: choosing to put aside the finite limits of a measured justice. It is a "going beyond" hurt and "moving into" mercy. This is what Micah, the Prophet, meant as he pleaded to God for mercy upon Israel:

> Who is a God like to thee, who takest away iniquity, and passest by the sin of the remnant of thy inheritance? he will send his fury in no more, because he delighteth in mercy. He will turn again, and have mercy on us: he will put away our iniquities: and he will cast all our sins into the bottom of the sea. (Mic 7:18-19)

It is difficult or impossible for the unredeemed, calloused soul to forgive. But you are His children; you have His Spirit: you have a renewed, reborn soul. Together, you and your spouse must pray that mercy will be a strong, steady attribute in your souls. Imitate Him with humble acts of mercy, and the power of love will course through your marriage with never-ending, refreshing waters flowing directly from God's eternal well.

Sabbath and Worship

The Lord's Day and The Sabbath

There is much that has been written and studied throughout the thousands of years concerning the sabbath. There is also much argument and confusion about the sabbath. As Roman Catholics, our understanding of the sabbath begins with the resurrection of our Lord Jesus Christ, The Lord's Day. We shall return to this later. First let us look in the Book of Exodus and see what is written:

> And the Lord spoke to Moses, saying: Speak to the children of Israel, and thou shalt say to them: See that thou keep my sabbath: because it is a sign between me and you in your generations: that you may know that I am the Lord, who sanctify you. Keep you my sabbath: for it is holy unto you: he that shall profane it, shall be put to death: he that shall do my work in it, his soul shall perish out of the midst of his people. Six days shall you do work: in the seventh day is the sabbath, the rest holy to the Lord. Every one that shall do any work on this day, shall die. Let the children of Israel keep the sabbath, and cele-

> brate it in their generations. It is an everlasting
> covenant Between me and the children of Israel,
> and a perpetual sign. For in six days the Lord
> made heaven and earth, and in the seventh he
> ceased from work. (Exod 31:12-17)

From the period when those scriptures were first taught until the day when Jesus began His ministry, the teachings on the sabbath "rest" became somewhat corrupted. It was in the latter period of Judaism that the Pharisees turned it into a dominant theological force. There is no doubt that it was the Love of God that offered the Israelite to rest with Him, consecrated to Him—to "draw breath with Him." These are Israelites, not pagans, not gentiles whom God called later. No matter how poor, how downtrodden, how much of a social outcast, all in Israel had that opportunity to rest and experience a pause and piety in life. There is a witty epigram written sometime in Asher Ginzberg's life (1856-1927): "More than the Jews have kept the sabbath, the sabbath has kept the Jews." And so to this day the sabbath is celebrated and set apart. The sabbath rest continues, but a rest under the law.

Now to the New Testament. There are numerous acts of compassion which the Apostles record throughout the Gospels showing Jesus healing on the sabbath. In the twelfth chapter of Matthew, the Pharisees confront Jesus regarding His Apostles who were picking corn—something forbidden on the sabbath. He responded, "And if you knew what this meaneth: I will have mercy, and not sacrifice: you would never have condemned the innocent. For the Son of man is Lord even of the sabbath" (Matt 12:7-8).

"For the Son of Man is Lord even of the sabbath." Our resurrected Lord is not only Lord of the sabbath; He is the Lord of all days. Do we see Jesus cancelling the sabbath? St. Paul, warning the Colossians against Judaizing Christians trying to impose on them the sabbath obligations, writes, "Let no man therefore judge you in meat or in drink, or in respect of a festival day, or of the new moon, or of the sabbaths, Which are a shadow of things to come, but the body is of Christ" (Col 2:16-17). Do we read that St. Paul cancelled the sabbath? No. He released the faithful from the obligations of observing the law.

As Roman Catholics, the Lord's Day, His resurrection, is our celebration. "Come to me, all you that labour, and are burdened, and I will refresh you. Take up my yoke upon you, and learn of me, because I am meek, and humble of heart: and you shall find rest to your souls" (Matt 11:28-29). A day of rest was set aside for the people of Israel, for them to make it holy. As Christians, we are called by Jesus to find our rest in Him. This world, which is being accelerated by technology, dragging and hurling the human spirit into the unknown and uncertain, offers very little to the faithful seeking rest. We must learn from our holy ancestors, the Saints, and our pious Jewish cousins, that properly resting with God is an act of His love which allows us to learn from Him how to Breathe with Him—so that we may be refreshed in spirit amidst a world afflicted with anxiety and uncertainty. Rest with our Risen Lord, and learn to breathe with Him.

The Holy Eucharist

> And whilst they were at supper, Jesus took bread, and blessed, and broke: and gave to his disciples, and said: Take ye, and eat. This is my body. And taking the chalice, he gave thanks, and gave to them, saying: Drink ye all of this. For this is my blood of the new testament, which shall be shed for many unto remission of sins. (Matt 26:26-28)

As Roman Catholics, we are taught that at that moment of Consecration, the bread and wine are no longer; they do not exist, though we still see the accidents—bread and wine. They are now the Body and Blood of Jesus Christ—a Mystery to many. In telling us a little about himself, Jesus states:

> I am the bread of life. Your fathers did eat manna in the desert, and are dead. This is the bread which cometh down from heaven; that if any man eat of it, he may not die. I am the living bread which came down from heaven. If any man eat of this bread, he shall live for ever; and

the bread that I will give, is my flesh, for the life
of the world. (John 6:48-52)[10]

When receiving the Holy Eucharist, imagining the Real Presence of Jesus, some people may see Him preaching, teaching, and healing as He does in the Holy Gospels. Others may imagine the resurrected Christ, whose appearances to different disciples give us various images of His resurrected body. Still others will always remember Him as the Suffering Servant, the Lamb of God.

But Jesus also exists within the Holy Eucharist in another way—as the Primordial/Pre-existent Christ. The earliest records and sacred scriptures of our Church teach us about the Primordial Christ—the Christ before everything began—and about the Pre-existent Christ—Christ the way He existed before entering humanity's salvation history, as the way the prophets saw Him. The Gospel of John begins by telling us of the Primordial Christ:

> In the beginning was the Word,
> and the Word was with God,
> and the Word was God.
> The same was in the beginning with God.
> All things were made by him:

---

[10] In the Latin Vulgate and the Douay-Rheims, these verses are numbered as verses 48-52 of John 6. In more recent translations, these verses are numbered as verses 48-51 of John 6.

and without him was made nothing that was made.
In him was life,
and the life was the light of men. (John 1:1-4)

In the Book of Daniel, the Prophet describes the Pre-existent Christ:

> I beheld therefore in the vision of the night,
> and lo, one like the son of man
> came with the clouds of heaven,
> and he came even to the Ancient of days:
> and they presented him before him.
> And he gave him power, and glory, and a kingdom:
> and all peoples, tribes and tongues shall serve him:
> his power is an everlasting power
> that shall not be taken away:
> and his kingdom that shall not be destroyed. (Dan 7:13-14)

Also, in the Book of Revelation, the Apostle John describes Him in imagery outside of man's understanding of time:

> And I turned to see the voice that spoke with me. And being turned, I saw seven golden candlesticks: And in the midst of the seven golden candlesticks, one like to the Son of man, clothed with a garment down to the feet, and girt about the paps with a golden girdle. And his head and

> his hairs were white, as white wool, and as snow, and his eyes were as a flame of fire, And his feet like unto fine brass, as in a burning furnace. And his voice as the sound of many waters. And he had in his right hand seven stars. And from his mouth came out a sharp two edged sword: and his face was as the sun shineth in his power. (Rev 1:12-16)

You may ask yourselves what does all of this have to do with the Holy Eucharist? Jesus Christ remains a Mystery to many. He continues to remain so to those whose faith is weak and diluted with the world's skepticism. The Apostle John tells us:

> He was in the world,
> and the world was made by him,
> and the world knew him not.
> He came unto his own,
> and his own received him not.
> But as many as received him,
> he gave them power to be made the sons of God... (John 1:10-12)

As faithful Roman Catholics, we are so blessed that our Holy Church is continually ascertaining and providing for our spiritual well-being as we grow into that grace-filled power. The centuries and centuries of revelations and catechesis handed down to us from illumined and Holy

Saints—such as St. Thomas Aquinas and his *Summa Theologica,* and Doctrine of Divine Transubstantiation and others—Popes and Councils, the Magisterium, and the Catechism of the Catholic Church, have more than revealed these inspired and grace-filled truths, gently leading us to the real Presence of His Body and Blood, Soul and Divinity—not only of our Lord as humanity experienced and recorded Him in the Gospels and New Testament Letters, but also of His Primordial/Pre-existent glory, as witnessed by His Prophets and the Apostle.

Let's imagine and review how the Prophet Daniel and the Apostle John described Him. Then let us travel in time, examining our scriptures, seeing Bethlehem, Joseph, Mary giving birth to her son, her firstborn, wrapping this little, crying, kicking-the-air uncircumcised infant...Who is the same exact person we see in the Prophet Daniel and the Book of Revelation—*The* Lord of Everlasting Glory, now wrapped in swaddling clothes. Jesus is a Mystery to some people. Jesus lived a hidden life. If you saw him as a ten year old, you would see twenty or thirty others like him in his village. At twenty years old, if he was in his house and you saw him through a window as you passed by, the only thing separating you from the Lord of Eternal Glory would be a wooden wall on a dusty street with wandering dogs and children chasing each other...

How profound! The Lord of Eternal Glory wrapped in the common human skin of a twenty-year-old human body with a growing beard—truly a hidden life! "He was in the world, and the world was made by him, and the world knew him not" (John 1:10).

If our God Jesus did that and rose from the dead, and we *know* He did, He can just as assuredly change Himself into the Body and Blood; though the bread and wine remain, they no longer exist. For the faithful who see and hear, Jesus is no longer a Mystery. He is God's Gift to us as Lord, a promise to rely upon because His resurrection nurtures the faith for the righteous to hope in. I don't think we can exactly know or number the amount of books, articles, encyclicals, essays, and the like which have been written about the Holy Eucharist. Nor can we know the amount of Eucharistic miracles which have occurred throughout the centuries.

"But as many as received him, he gave them power to be made the sons of God..." (John 1:12).

In the previous chapters, I wrote, saying marriage is between husband, wife, and God. We have access to Jesus through the Holy Spirit and prayer. We have access to Jesus through the Holy Eucharist, which presents us with His Body and Blood, His Soul and Divinity. Our sacrament of marriage in Christ is blessed with such rich graces because of His Presence within the being of each spouse. By joining ourselves to the Holy Eucharist, we grow into the marital miracle of oneness. Marriage is the Miracle where two become one in Christ.

The way He was hidden within the common flesh of a twenty year old, in that same way—during the consecration—He is gloriously hidden within the non-existing substance of ordinary wheat and wine. Jesus comes unto His own and they know Him. When I see some of our Church's elderly bent over with age and partially crippled bodies with pained arthritic hands awaiting the receiving of His Presence, I always think of them offering their sufferings to Him. Although when receiving Him they still walk away with pain-ridden hands, they also walk away with a visit from the Everlasting Lord of Glory who blesses, though hidden, in their obedient, humble, and faith-filled hearts. I imagine His Body becoming one with their bodies infusing health and strength; His Blood becoming one with their blood, purging their blood from all stain of sin. I also see His Soul entering their souls and the holiness of His Heart purifying their hearts that in faith they may see Him and the Holiness of His Father's Presence with Him. Lastly, because we are created in the likeness and image of Him, when His Divinity enters into us, it will spark our struggling hopes to see and live Love Divine. As Roman Catholics, we are richly blessed when we live His promises with our developing gifts of faith.

Let us never forget what St. Paul states to the Colossians:

> Therefore, if you be risen with Christ, seek the
> things that are above; where Christ is sitting at

> the right hand of God: Mind the things that are above, not the things that are upon the earth. For you are dead; and your life is hid with Christ in God. When Christ shall appear, who is your life, then you also shall appear with him in glory. (Col 3:1-4)

As spouses, we should always remember that while this hidden process of salvation happens and Jesus is busy in us during Holy Communion, our marriage is being doubly graced and strengthened: first, by the active purity and love we each have for the other; and secondly, by the reality that He is Present and our faith believes and confirms His Presence. So what God has wondrously united in the Sacrament of Matrimony, He continues to holily unite and perfect in and through the Holy Eucharist. This is a glimpse with which we can envision our Powerful and Mighty God, yet tender in Mercy, and full of Divine Love, hidden, though gloriously and powerfully present to the family of faith, with their desiring souls and others with twisted painful bodies. No one can see Him. Not even the person He visited. He continues to remain hidden, in compassion and Love, in and through a Holy Eucharistic moment.

Conclusion

I have addressed only a fraction of the trials and challenges you may encounter in your Christian marriage. However, be assured that the spiritual unity of "marital oneness" is God's gift to mankind. The blessings which await the pure in heart within a faithful union in Christ far exceed the havoc the devil intends when attempting to put asunder what God has joined.

I pray that what I have written will provide a little wellspring of grace as you discover the seriousness and profound possibilities of the commitment involved in a lasting and joyful marriage. Remember that no two marital experiences are identical. Be thankful for who you and your spouse are as individuals and for the unique spiritual identity your love creates. God never duplicates the marital makeup of two people in love.

Do not forget that throughout all of history since the creation of Adam and Eve, never did the proud in heart occupy a permanent station within God's will, light, and love. Therefore, walk softly in this noisy world, calm yourselves and your souls, discipline your marital conduct, be humble with your thoughts and deeds, seek to serve rather than just to be served. Let your marriage and family be fulfilled in the life and fruition of the Christian faith.

Most importantly, love God freely with joy and intensity, and pursue virtue. Love your spouse as you love yourself and take the marriage of Christ to His Bride, the Church, as your example. Lastly, remember: what God has joined together, He can keep together. Christ began His ministry of miracles with the marriage in Cana. Offer your marriage to Him, and you too will see a miracle manifested in your lives, and you will journey forward together, best friends, united in the joy and wonder of His Love, Presence, and Glory.

May the blessings of our Lord be forever upon you.

Questions for Self-Examination

1. The Soul (31):

    How can I get to know my soul better?

2. Singleness of Heart (39):

    How can I become more aware of the intentions and desires of my heart, so as to fix my heart more steadily and deeply on the true treasures which should be there?

3. Prayer (43):

    Is my prayer life insincere, shallow, infrequent? If my answer is yes, what can I do to improve sincerity, depth, and regularity of prayer?

4. Grace (45):

    As baptized Christians we are God's children living in a state of grace—sanctifying and actual. Do we understand how to access the "graces" available to assist us, not only with our redemption, but more specifically, with our marriage?

5. Devotion (47):

   What steps can I take to more deeply experience the empowerment of "devotion" to God, to my spouse, and to marriage?

6. Communication (51):

   In mutual respect, do we have an open and genuine communication experience regardless of the sensitivity of issues? If not, how can we nurture this experience?

7. Change (55):

   Recognizing danger signals threatening marital unity, am I capable of humbling myself and being flexible, so "change" may come about and create the direction needed to stabilize our marriage?

8. Peace and Tranquility (59):

   Have I ever experienced the peace of Christ? If my answer is no, what can I do to acquire that "special" peace even when burdensome trials are at hand?

9. Trust (63):

   What are the three things that I can do to learn to increase trust for my spouse?

10. Fear (67):

    When we seem to be overwhelmed by fears of all sorts, do we realize that in order to truly meet and confront those fears, we need to have a biblical understanding of "the fear of the Lord" in our daily lives, at all times? What disciplines can we practice and adopt to help us trust in, rely on, shelter, and rest in Jesus while dealing with those fears?

11. Vision (73):

    Have we ever discussed a "vision" for our marriage? If the answer is no, why haven't we? And how can we begin to develop one?

12. Faith and Reason (77):

    When attempting to make decisions, do I try to apply both an educated faith and balanced reasoning, and do I include my spouse in that process?

13. Human Sexuality (81):

    Is our understanding of the mystery of Human Sexuality in alignment with Biblical teachings that our bodies are temples of the Holy Spirit? As such, our conduct should reflect the fact that God is our creator and author in this joyful mystery of love and creation. If we are doubtful, what can we do to align our experiences to allow us the freedom to grow in peace and lawful sexual joy with each other in Christ?

14. The Marriage Bed (85):

    Is my marital sexual experience without stain? Is it free from pre-marital shadows? Is it healthy, wholesome, and exciting? If my answer is doubtful, what can I do to bring about a healthy and vibrant sexual experience with my spouse?

15. Friendship (91):

    Have I genuinely discovered that "best friend" in my spouse? If my answer is no, what three things can I do to promote that special friendship?

16. Long-Suffering (95):

    Am I permitting Christ and the unfailing power of His love—the mightiest of His forces—to share and endure my most burdening times with me? If my answer is no, what can I do to include and increase my awareness of Jesus' help during my trying moments?

17. Encouragement in Trials and Temptations (99):

    When experiencing temptations or trials, do I know enough about the "roots" of my faith to encourage myself to persevere in the goodness of God's truth? If my answer is no, what can I do to better educate myself about the development of spiritual "roots"?

18. Finances (103):

    Am I being financially responsible to my/our obligations? Do we have an operating budget or a financial plan acceptable to both?

19. Pleasure (107):

    Am I enjoying pleasures pleasing to my spouse and to God? Are we mutually enjoying and sharing pleasures pleasing to both of us?

20. Lukewarm Love (111):

    Is my love for my spouse lukewarm, indifferent, or noncaring? If my answer is yes, what three things I can do, with God's help, to enrich and intensify our shared love?

21. Competitiveness (115):

    Do I support, encourage, and inspire my spouse to higher achievements? Or am I contending and striving with him/her and possibly canceling what could have otherwise been a fruitful and beneficial experience?

22. Meanness (117):

    When bitterness becomes the prevailing mood for the moment, what can I do in that moment to prevent an ill temper from overtaking the rest of my senses thereby offending and hurting my spouse?

23. Doubt (119):

    What are some spiritual practices I can apply to become a more sure-minded Christian, thereby eliminating doubt from hindering my growth in Christ?

24. Evil Thoughts (121):

    When being confronted by evil attractions, how can I, with grace, prevent myself from indulging in evil thoughts which could upset and injure my relationship with my spouse?

25. Rejection (123):

    As a person with complicated needs and a desire to be loved, how can I overcome the emotions of being rejected?

26. The Pain of Disappointment (127):

    Have I satisfactorily handled the pain of disappointment in a mature Christian manner? Or have I brooded with the "poor me," self-pity attitude? Have I taken that disappointment to the Lord and trusted Him to lead me forward?

27. Anger (129):

    When I get angry, do I look at myself, as well as my spouse—and if either or both of us are responsible for the cause of anger, how can we prepare ourselves to seek forgiveness—from each other and God?

28. Vanity (133):

    What can I do to reveal the "true me" and avoid wearing masks which determine vain roles that falsely mislead me from my true identity as a loving person as well as a son or daughter of the Lord?

29. Married Image and Appearance (137):

    How can I avoid being hypocritical by wearing two faces—one face when with my spouse, the other when apart from him/her, and in the world?

30. Separation and Reconciliation (141):

    If irresponsible or sinful behavior ruptured and bruised the unity of marital love, how can we correct ourselves to reestablish that peace and unity?

31. Cultural Differences (145):

    When we encounter conflict with each other, do we stop to ask ourselves if the disagreement might be due in whole or in part to the different cultural lenses through which each of us is looking?

32. Children (149):

    Our children's identity and destinies lie in God. What can we do as faithful parents and stewards to help them realize their potential for a life experienced daily in Grace?

33. Reading (153):

    Do we share with each other the thoughts, reflections, and wonderings God gives to us each day? Have we considered a specific time for this sharing?

34. In-Laws (157):

    When we talk about our son/daughter-in-law or mother/father-in-law, do we first remember that we are eternally bound to the duties of kindness, truth, and spiritual respect?

35. Forgiveness (161):

    When I need to forgive, do I go into my private chamber and ask the Lord to create forgiveness in me and the capacity to truly let go of bitterness and to seek to understand?

36. Sabbath and Worship (165):

    What, for me, is Sabbath rest? What is rest for my spouse? How can we spend more Sabbath time experiencing these truly restful and refreshing activities together?

37. The Holy Eucharist (169):

    Does my faith allow me to fully appreciate and enter into the Mystery, the real presence of Jesus Christ in the Holy Eucharist? If my answer is no, how can I grow into a fuller appreciation and deeper experience of this sacred Mystery?

Made in United States
Orlando, FL
03 October 2023